MW01618696

INTELLIGENCE GAMES FOR YOUR WHOLE FAMILY

50+ Fun Activities for Awareness, Empathy, Emotional Control, and other Social Skills

TIFFANY WAYNE

Interior illustrations by Saba Azeem

Published by Cothan Global Inc.,

22 Mogul Drive, North York, Ontario, Canada M2H2M7

ISBN: 978-1-7781366-2-7 (ebook)

ISBN: 978-1-7781366-0-3 (Paperback)

ISBN: 978-1-7781366-1-0 (Hardcover)

First printing, 2022

To Ethan and Connor, my sonshines

I love you to infinity and beyond.

CONTENTS

INTRODUCTION

Emotional intelligence. It sounds like an oxymoron, one of those seemingly inherently contradictory phrases, like *jumbo shrimp* or *poor little rich girl*. Aren't emotion and intellect mutually exclusive? No, and in fact no oxymoron is strictly paradoxical. They're based on wordplay, verbal riddles like *military intelligence*, designed to amuse and nothing else.

But there are two oxymorons that are no joke, and they're both printed on the cover of this book. Besides *emotional intelligence*, there's another: Whole Family. The modern family is under attack, assaulted by countless new pressures that previous generations didn't face; sometimes it is all we can do to defuse conflict, head off angst, and stop our families from fracturing and fragmenting.

If that rings true for you, improved attention to emotional intelligence might just help you and your family. But there's more to it than that. With the internet, smartphones, and two- (or more-) income households, there is less and less time for traditional family togetherness. Technology has brought people from disparate corners of the world together in an instant, but it drives people in the same household further apart. Anybody who has ever seen each member of their family staring into their smartphone, even while sitting in the same room, knows what this is all about.

And that's the most docile aspect of it. The internet has brought a stream of influences into the average home which parents increasingly cannot manage. This results in identity crises in children who are most susceptible to it. At the same time, parents are working harder for less and have less time and attention for the increasingly maladjusted children of their increasingly fractured homelife.

The problems develop hand-in-hand, one thing working off the other in a spiral that can project downward, or upward. Fewer opportunities for interaction create family disunity, which results in inattentive parenting and unguided child development, the sum total of which is less emotional intelligence in the family overall. On the other hand, more opportunity for interaction creates unity, which leads to more attentive parenting and more well-guided child development, the sum total of which is greater emotional intelligence in the family overall.

IS EMOTIONAL INTELLIGENCE TRULY THAT IMPORTANT?

High emotional intelligence (also called EQ) is often closely linked to high IQ. Children who exhibit high levels of emotional intelligence tend to perform better on most standardized tests. They often earn higher grades.

High emotional intelligence notably leads to better relationships. The skills developed through higher emotional intelligence are invaluable to establishing and managing long-term relationships and friendships. It's central to proper socialization.

Emotional intelligence is also key to success in personal and professional arenas later in life. Studies show that children who are able to share and cooperate and follow directions by the age of five are more likely to get their college degrees and work full-time jobs by the age of 25.

Children with more emotional intelligence have been shown to have overall improved mental health in childhood and adulthood, including avoiding depression.

Scary statistics tell another tale. As recently as 2019:

- Roughly 50% of married couples had received marriage counseling
- Marriage counseling had had a success rate of about 70%
- 13.6% of children in the U.S. between five and 17 years of age had received mental health treatment in the last year
- 10.0% of children had received counseling and/or therapy
- 8.4% had taken prescription mental health medication
- There were over 30,000 marriage and family therapists in the United States
- The job growth for marriage and family therapists in the U.S. had grown by over 22% in the last ten years

So yes, there's a problem. But isolating the problem is only half the battle. Luckily, this is a battle which will not be 'fought' at all. In fact, it's a war to be won by *not* fighting. It's the fighting which caused the war in the first place, but it resulted in lack of communication. So, the solution to poorly adjusted children and poorly developed family bonds is emotional intelligence, but improving emotional intelligence is made harder by weakened family ties.

SO, HOW DO WE WIN THE BATTLE? NOT BY FIGHTING, BUT BY PLAYING.

We humbly suggest that grand tradition: game night. There was a time when families were together for the evening. Children didn't go out unsupervised. There were no movies to go to. Families listened to the radio together if they had one. They gathered around the piano and sang. They worked together, they played together, and they developed stronger bonds.

True, those were different times, and there's no going back to the world of churning butter and riding horse carts. Still, we can take a page from that time and bring it into our own world. Many families already institute one family meal a week to keep these bonds strong. And when your kids are young, as they will largely be for these games, they'll naturally be home more. Those are formative years which should be exploited to develop these crucial skills and bonds.

And you can do them both at once.

These games are fun and easy to play, with little preparation. True, there are games out there for kids, overpriced boxes with colored cards which have one game only. We offer dozens. One game may be good for children of a certain age, but we have games for kids of all ages, even hard-to-please older kids. Other games are meant for children to play with one another, while these games are designed to be played by the family. Family time can take on new, positive associations instead of the dreaded arguments or lectures or other unpleasant artifacts of a lack of emotional intelligence. You can make memories while you teach invaluable lessons, which will not only help you and your children every day of their lives, but will likely change their lives forever.

And they're fun, for you as well as for the kids. As an adult, you may have lost your sense of whimsy. And that's a shame. There are innumerable benefits to letting your guard down, especially in front of your children. It can reduce stress at the end of the day. Having a more tranquil household will certainly reduce your stress!

Some of the benefits of using these games with your family, and understanding and even mastering the principles behind them, will be instant, short-term, and long-term for you all, including:

- Individual personality development
- Friendship building
- Increased mutual respect

- Greater obedience
- Fewer temper tantrums

Once again, those things are not unique to children. Maybe you're the one prone to temperamental outbursts, and maybe your child is learning that from you. Learn more about the person you are, and you'll know more about the person you should be. And don't forget the old adage: We become our parents. Even as you'll be leading the games, you'll also be learning the lessons too.

The book has a hidden benefit as well. If you are a manager of any group of people, these games can be tailored to your work team. You will find all the same benefits there as you will be playing these games in your home with your family. So really, you're reading two books in one. Who knows, you may find other ways of applying the same principles. If you're the coach of a sports team, emotional intelligence and team unity are crucial. If you're a teacher and can work this into your curriculum with your administration's blessings, you will find your children infinitely more engaged and receptive and well-socialized. They're great for relationships too, romantic or otherwise.

What you won't get will be a volume of statistics, historical timelines, names of European psychologists, or the results of university studies. There are other books for those things, and we highly recommend them if you're doing a master's in child or family psychology. But what we offer is going to be much more practical. Of course, there will be some background information you'll need, and a brief survey of what we're doing and why. Don't worry, it's not rocket science. You probably already know a lot of it instinctively.

Nevertheless, we reassure you that these are time-tested applications designed for the age groups which categorize them. They are based on the most modern psychological research (which is growing all the time). So, rest assured that you're in good hands.

With that comes the caveats which are to come. This is your family and the choices you make are your responsibility. We're here to give you as many choices as we can, what we believe are the best choices.

But a little information will go a long way. Much of what you will learn, and what you will teach, will become clear as we go.

You'll also find just a little bit of good humor. These are games, after all, not laboratory experiments. So a little bit of fun is baked into the cake. But don't mistake the work for frivolous. The welfare of your family is our primary objective here. And don't expect a new book by the likes of Jeff Foxworthy. It's not a joke book.

And speaking seriously, let's toss out a few caveats, too: These games are designed to identify and correct 'blind spots' or 'areas of improvement' in our emotional intelligence. If they alert you to what could be deep-rooted issues, be advised that this book is not a substitute for formal therapy, if that is required. These fun games may help you avoid that, or they may reveal the need for it, but they won't cure any fundamental developmental problems. There are lots of qualified therapists who will be eager and able to take up your cause and fight your corner.

Along these lines, don't feel like you've got to play every game, of course. Certain games will be more effective than others for certain kids. But that doesn't mean you should only play the games which are the least challenging. On the contrary, retry the ones that don't work the first time. Try not to try a game twice in a row, whether or not it is effective or revealing or fun. But if you repeat a game (not twice in a row) and your family doesn't take to it, forget it. There are plenty of others. Too many bad experiences will turn your kids off to the whole practice, and that would be a terrible shame. They need the development this book offers, just about everyone does. They may well need it quite desperately, or *you* may.

Also, you'll need little more than a few common household objects, but here are a few you might want to keep handy:

- A ball to toss
- A walnut
- Paper
- Pen or pencil
- Wipe board
- Colored markers
- A large bowl or hat
- Scissors
- The internet-
- A computer and printer
- A stereo
- A TV and DVD player

A lot of it is about picking words out of a hat and making lists. The internet and computer equipment (the bare minimum is needed here) is for finding pictures and printing them. Other than that, your imaginations will do a lot of the heavy lifting.

Enjoy!

PART ONE

Chapter 1:

What is Emotional Intelligence?

Emotional intelligence is loosely defined as an ability to perceive, regulate, and manage emotions, your own and those of other people. It was commonly thought that emotional intelligence was, like intellectual intelligence, innate, and could not be learned or taught, though it could be developed. But emotional intelligence is just a turn of phrase, and must be treated that way. It could just as easily be emotional awareness, and awareness can certainly be learned and developed; it has to be for a well-developed individual and a well-functioning community and society.

A person who has mastered emotional intelligence exhibits these traits:

- Awareness of the roots and causes of their own emotional impulses
- Awareness of the trigger circumstances associated with which emotional impulses
- Willingness to alter trigger circumstances associated with emotional impulses

- Willingness to learn more about the roots, causes, triggers, and further alterations
- Awareness of the roots and causes of others' emotional impulses
- Awareness of the trigger circumstances associated with others' emotional impulses
- Willingness to alter trigger circumstances associated with others' emotional impulses
- Willingness to learn more about the roots, causes, triggers, and further alterations of others' emotional impulses
- Willingness to engage in active listening

Note that emotional intelligence is not just about understanding these things, but being willing to change one's behavior in accordance with that understanding. If a person knows that what they are doing is antisocial or unhealthy or unsound, but does not take steps to change their behavior, that is considered disordered behavior. There are volumes on personality disorders, but again, that's not the primary focus of this book. However, we certainly can say that highly developed emotional intelligence, predicated on a strong sense of empathy and developed early in life, will reduce the likelihood of anybody developing harmful personality disorders later in life. It's also noteworthy that a lot of personality disorders begin to develop in the teenage and pre-teenage years, so instilling emotional intelligence early on is highly recommended to establish a healthy psyche. That's not to say it can't be developed later in life if necessary.

ACTIVE LISTENING

A moment is required here to discuss the concept of active listening. In short, active listening entails, well, actively listening. Active listening entails:

- Paying attention
- Focusing on the other person, not on yourself
- Ridding your mind of distraction
- Not interrupting
- Processing information
- Imprinting information using repetition and paraphrasing
- Using information to formulate other related summations
- Using information to problem-solve

Basically, active listening means you're not just sitting there, nodding and smiling and thinking about your next quip. It means you're paying attention, that you're actively involved with what the other person is saying.

Active listening is paramount to good communications skills, leadership skills, social skills, and of course, emotional intelligence. Emotional intelligence is about understanding and coping with the emotions of others (as well as your own). But how better to understand what inspires the emotions of others around you than to pay attention when they share about themselves? You'll want to solicit that information, and you'll surely want to remember it. That will help you identify and avoid their triggers, even if they can't do so themselves. But, of course, if we're talking about children, they will probably not share an adult's high emotional intelligence!

Active listening means you care; it means you're not always thinking only of yourself. It means you have empathy, and that is crucial to emotional intelligence, in addition to so many other vital skill sets.

WHY IS EMOTIONAL INTELLIGENCE IMPORTANT?

Some of the benefits of emotional intelligence include:

- Less stress
- Increased self-respect
- Better health
- Wider social circles
- Wider professional circles
- Greater success

The emotionally intelligent are not wrestling with their own emotions. They rarely have emotional conflicts with others, and they make and keep friends. They impress those in a position to give them opportunities. They have dynamic social and romantic lives. The power of emotional intelligence in romance is off the charts, but that's not quite our focus here! Again, volumes have been written, and this is a book about family.

Conversely, those who lack emotional intelligence are noted for:

- Social isolation
- Depression
- Low self-respect
- Poor diet and health
- Stymied social lives
- Stymied professional opportunities

Those who lack emotional intelligence may be emotionally erratic themselves and have contentious relationships with others. This may frustrate them socially, which can hobble a person's personal development with self-medication, poor diet, reduced self-esteem, professional failure, depression, and a whole host of other problems.

Having a mastery of emotional intelligence, or lacking one, can send a person on a trajectory for lifetime happiness or misery. Of course, the person with emotional intelligence will at least know why, while the other may never gain any insight.

Awareness.

MINDFULNESS

When we think of awareness, we're really talking about mindfulness, which is central to emotional intelligence. It's about being measured in our perceptions and our behavior. This whole book is predicated on the notion that emotional intelligence can be learned and developed, as these are the goals of the book: to help you develop emotional intelligence in your children, in yourselves, and to create stronger family bonds. You'll also have some fun, and who doesn't want that with the family?

Mindfulness can apply to a number of behaviors, including:

- Physical caution
- Politeness
- Appreciation
- Communal support
- Lack of physical aggression
- Deliberate use of reason
- Empathy

You'll note the commonality of these traits: All include interaction with another person (or element in a few cases). A person who is mindful is aware of another person's feelings when they are polite and supportive. They are mindful of the importance of reason over emotion and manage their own physical aggression. They may be cautious of dangerous elements like antisocial behavior, which also requires an active awareness of other people. The whole of our society, of any society, is predicated on some manner of awareness of the rights of others and the reasons for those rights.

Empathy can be loosely described as a sensitivity to the emotions of others. It allows us to feel what others feel, and that helps us to understand different perspectives. That is crucial to emotional intelligence, which includes understanding the emotions of others. Emotions are generated by people, and they reveal a lot about those people (for social purposes, too much). So, to understand people and deal with them effectively, one has to have empathy. And empathy is like mindfulness to the max!

CAN EMOTIONAL INTELLIGENCE BE TAUGHT?

Like the whole idea of emotional intelligence, there is a question as to whether or not empathy can be taught. There are volumes about the nature versus nurture argument and how it applies to psychology, and this book isn't about that kind of in-depth study. So, as promised, we'll be brief.

Most things are a combination of nature and nurture.

Boom, problem solved.

True, some people have a naturally stronger sense of empathy, some do not. There are traits of temperament which differ from person to person. Just as people are all different, there are also variations in cultures. But these individuals share common influences, either in a shared household, community, or country. External events (nurture) accentuate internal strengths or weaknesses (nature) and those things develop accordingly. The internal soon affects the external, which affects the internal in a cycle of nature and nurture. It's no longer adequate to excuse most behaviors in either children or adults. *That's just the way we are*, is no longer acceptable.

THE CYCLE OF BEHAVIOR

As long as we're looking at the internal, this is something that everybody who seeks to master emotional intelligence must understand. There is a three-step cycle of behavior in human beings. If all three steps are present and fully developed, that person's behavior is likely to be ordered. If they are in the wrong order, or some are skipped, and this is the case in the vast majority of people, that behavior will be disordered. The behavioral cycle is:

- Emotion
- Thought
- Action

After any external stimulus, the very first thing that happens in the psyche is emotion. This is the primary reaction in animals, in mammals particularly. Whether it is lust, fear, anger, or glee, emotion is the first thing that happens.

Thought follows quickly. Emotions are combined with memories and core values. This leads to a decision of action. People rarely act without thinking, even if only for a split-second.

The problem is that a split-second isn't enough for emotion or thought or action. People are not deliberate about this cycle, and it results in antisocial behavior. It also prevents emotional intelligence. A person who hardly feels and only thinks may act in a manner which is cold and lacking in concern for others. A person who feels (a selfish process generally) and does not think about others before acting is also exhibiting disordered, antisocial behavior. A person who thinks, then acts, and then feels afterwards is also getting it wrong. It's a simple thing to understand but an easy thing to overlook.

EMOTION AND REASON

An important note about the cycle of behavior described above is that it features emotions (feeling) and reason (thought). These two work together in a kind of duality we often see (think of the Ying and the Yang). Every human psyche has feelings (emotions) and thoughts (reason). Both are crucial to a well-adjusted psyche. They often influence one another to some degree, before action occurs. Social actions result from a balance of emotions and reason, and antisocial actions result from an imbalance of emotions and reason.

But it is important to be mindful that one will prevail over the other. It is common and it is contagious that people act based on their emotions, setting reason aside. But when acting and behaving in a social arena (any interaction between two or more people), reason must always prevail. Balance is found upon reflection, and upon reflection it is reason which prevails. It is the nature of emotion to occur first, but to pass. Reason remains consistent, based on facts which are stable when returned to for further scrutiny. So when people act fast (really, just reacting), they are acting out of emotion. When they respond in time, they are generally acting with reason as their central focus, not emotion. And when you or anybody is interacting socially, reason should always prevail. The two cannot prevail at the same time in the same human psyche. We'll see how all this figures into making the lives of you and your family better. But for now, keep these things in mind.

EMOTIONAL INTELLIGENCE IN CHILDREN AND ADULTS

Since this is a book about families, and is basically a collection of games for families to develop emotional intelligence (as well as to strengthen familial bonds), let's take a quick look at the nature of EI as it applies to adults and to children.

The tenets of each are the same. But the manifestations of these behaviors differ. How do you know if your child lacks emotional intelligence? How do you know if you do? Wait, you aren't the child, are you? If you are, good for you for reading this book! Whoever you are, the facts are the same. But children are not adults, and they will naturally lack emotional intelligence to a greater degree. It will change their behavior in different ways.

Lack of emotional intelligence in both adults and children manifests as:

- Depression
- Aggression
- Regression

But depression is harder to spot in children, who cannot express themselves. Parents often take this for temperament, like shyness. It expresses itself in adult or childlike recreational abuses which can be tragically similar (drugs and alcohol for both) or radically different (video games and social media, dark psychology for adults). Regression is easier to spot in children, whose development is easier to chart and comes in notable stages, whereas it does not in adults. But adults do this too, the infamous *midlife crisis* being the foremost example. Aggression is easier to spot in both adults and children, but passive aggression is more common in adults than children, the latter more often expressing unfettered aggression.

If any of this sounds familiar, there is probably a lack of emotional intelligence somewhere in your home. And let's face it, even those who have some emotional intelligence can always use a tune-up. Mindfulness is deliberate, but these things may slip with time and inattention.

Well, that's just about all you need to know. There's more to it, of course. But if you and your family have mastered everything in this chapter, roughly 2,000 words, you will be a beacon of well-adjusted behavior for the whole neighborhood. But since you bought this book, you can probably already isolate a few problem patterns emerging, in your children or in yourself. And, as we discussed in the introduction, you're looking for a way to improve these things in your family. You're looking to do it in a way which brings your family together.

Well, we've got what you've come for. So now that you have a solid understanding of what we're all doing, let's get to work … or play, as the case may be. Mutual trust, empathy, social interaction, developing family bonds: These are the foci of the games that follow.

PART TWO

Emotional Intelligence Games For Your Whole Family

Chapter 2

Games for Young Kids (Ages 4-7)

It's important to note that the very young can't be expected to have much emotional intelligence. In the first few years, human children are almost all emotion. Kids don't really become what we think of as being self-aware until they're about four or five, so this is the age to start making them aware of their emotions, what brings them on and how to control them.

But as regards the cycle of behavior, kids before four are all emotion and action, no thought to either one. Here is where thought begins and should be nurtured, but expect much more reliance upon emotion than thought before action for kids of this age.

These games are going to rely more on speaking and less on writing, as this is a skill many young kids are still developing.

INDOORS

THE BYE-BYE GAME:

This is great for children who may have separation anxiety, or are showing signs of it. It's a very common problem at early ages, especially for only children. But since separation anxiety is absolutely the dominance of emotion over reason, it's an early red flag of a lack of or need for greater emotional intelligence.

Play in any room of the house. Suggest that you play *The Bye-Bye Game* (say it this way so your child will be confident and positive going in). Sit them down and tell them you're going to go out for a moment. Tell them that, if they miss you, to shout out the silliest word they can think of. This teaches them, in a fun way, to associate feelings with words and to learn how to express their emotions with words (thoughts) before putting them into action (crying, perhaps).

On the first round, step out of the room, but before you close the door, return and shout out some crazy word of your own choice. Hug and kiss and reassure your child. This demonstrates that leaving will have a positive result, a loving return.

Try it again, but this time close the door and stay out of the room for, say, five seconds. Whether they call out their own word or not, return and say your own goofy word. Then hug and reassure. If they ask why you didn't wait, tell them that you missed them. That reassures them that their feelings are mutual and natural and nothing to be afraid of. Extend the period of your absence longer and longer as the game requires.

As your child matures, turn this into a game of hide and seek, which will have even greater effects on their sense of curiosity, engagement, and playful fun with their parents. That will resonate with them later, and with you.

Huggy Jail:

Here's a fun version of a classic monster chase game, but not as scary for young kids. Proclaim that the Huggy Thief (the child) is on the run, then chase them down. The punishment, of course, is a short stay in Huggy Jail, where you hug and kiss them. This encourages them to run free instead of being clingy, which is a sign of emotional unintelligence, if you will. It also demonstrates that you are there to look out for them, and that not all ramifications are negative. This will help with their ability to face challenges later in life.

To keep this game lively, and to allow it to keep up with your maturing children, allow them to turn around and chase you and put you in Huggy Jail. It's as much fun for you as it is for them.

Making Faces:

Here's a great game to play with your young children. This is a great way to play on their strengths and to excite both their imaginations and their communications skills. If you have more than one child, it's one you all can play together, so nobody has to wait for their turn, another aspect tailored to young children.

Simply collect their attention (which you'll do at the beginning of every game). To begin, pick an emotion, and have everybody make a face which best exemplifies that emotion. You will participate and lead by example (as in all of these games for younger kids). And let your example be exaggerated and comical, as much as you can. And you can! You've been making funny faces at your kids for a while, but now you're doing it with a purpose. The more they enact the facial expression, the more they will feel that emotion. Feel free to have everyone use their arms and posture, though have them remain seated for this exercise.

This game, like most, is meant to illicit fun and amusement during the process of learning. So don't shy away from laughing and enjoying it. When was the last time you and your family sat around with each other laughing?

Popular emotions for this game include:

- Happiness
- Sadness
- Anger
- Surprise
- Shyness
- Confusion
- Curiosity
- Frustration

Take note of your children's reactions. Are they slow to respond, are they grandly theatrical? Do they laugh with others, their siblings, or at them? Are they mutually supportive?

MAKING FACES

Take a closer look. When they illustrate frustration or anger or even joy, do they direct that at one another? Does one sibling hear anger and turn to their younger or older sibling? When they hear joy, which parent do they look at or enact toward? We're not trying to create rivalries between parents, of course. But if you've ever worried that maybe you're not connecting as closely with one child, this may be revealing. Along those lines, who are you enacting toward for anger or joy or suspicion? Your spouse? Your child? Which one?

This simple game becomes an exemplary exercise in emotional intelligence, which is primarily concerned with knowing how your own emotions interact in a social context. Who inspires which emotions in you? That's a trigger element, and something you'll have to look at and adapt to if you're to be well-adjusted and emotionally intelligent.

Naming Faces:

Here's a simple fix and a simple advance on the previous game. This time, go around from person to person, each of whom will enact an emotion and others guess which emotion that is. Since your children may not be of age to be reading and writing smoothly, feel free to let them pick one off the top of their heads. Use the same emotions you've used before. As the game leader, feel free to whisper some suggestions into a child's ear if they can't think of one. This cheat works best if there are more than just the two of you!

You can alter the rules if you have two kids and you want to have one act and the other guess, and you can support each player if they're too young to improvise and you want to keep things fair.

Making Faces And Bodies:

In the same way you made faces to describe emotions, try it this time in a place where you have a bit more room. You can play *Making Faces* over the dinner table, if you wish. This time, go into the living room or family room and make yourselves comfortable. Pick an emotion and, as the game leader, act the emotion out. You can use your face, but rely on your body, your body language. Do not speak during this game if you are enacting the emotion, but the guessers can call out their guesses at will. What actions convey frustration, maybe (pantomiming) pulling out your hair. What actions convey sorrow or joy? Don't hold back. And make sure to announce your emotion at the end so your younger children understand the full connection between your expression, that emotion, and the word associated with that emotion.

Emotions Charades:

Here we carry the previous game one step further. Pick an emotion and enact it, and instead of announcing it, let the observers call out their guesses. This is a good game for pre-teens as well. As with every version of Charades, no words are allowed from the person acting out the riddle.

The Hokey Pokey, Emotional Edition:

This is a great game for younger kids for so many reasons. It's one of the few singalong games we have, and kids love that. It's participatory, and kids love that. And they already know the song and how it works, and kids love that too.

So start this version the way you might end the standard version, which usually goes from feet to head and then whole self. This time, start with the head, then do the whole self. This is for several very specific reasons. For practical purposes, there's not enough time and juvenile attention to work your way up the whole body; that's a different version of the same song. You're establishing that the primary source is the head (which it is for both feelings and thoughts, as we know). Next, your whole self establishes that everything in your body is affected by everything in your head. The two things are directly connected, but the head is primary.

These two familiar contributions to the song push us right to the heart of the next verses, if you will.

Next, instead of putting your leg or arm in, you put your emotion in. Physically this means leaning forward just a bit and acting out the emotion in as straightforward a manner as possible (so kids can learn them easily and quickly). Try these:

- **Sad:** Flexing your fists in front of your eyes to denote crying
- **Happy:** Wide smiles and opened eyes, jazz hands

- **Tired:** Slouching posture (this is a good substitute for depression for kids of this age)

You can also substitute emotions for behaviors, as the connection between these two is important to establish in a child's mind:

- **Mean:** A snarl
- **Sweet:** Batting your eyes
- **Fun:** A silly face
- **Grouchy:** Crossing your arms in front of your chest
- **Silly:** Stick your tongue out, make a goofy face (a la Harpo Marx)

This game teaches children that emotions are just as much a part of them as their arms or legs, that they're just as necessary. And just as the traditional version of the song teaches kids to identify (arms, legs) and group (left, right) using parts of their body, the new version teaches them the same thing, to identify (mad, sweet) and group (emotions, traits). It also combines the elements of *Making Faces* into a song-and-dance format which young kids can hardly resist.

Coloring Emotions:

Kids love coloring, so here's a great way to appeal to their sense of artistic expression. It could lead them to all manner of fruitful endeavors and mindfulness later in life. We'll be coming back to this concept in later games, and you'll notice we often return to principles we visit in these games for younger children. In fact, as your children grow older, you'll probably be coming back to these principles and this book to keep this tradition alive and developing them as your family matures.

This time, spread out some colored markers (or crayons if you prefer) and paper. Acquaint your children with the rules and purpose, like this:

"You know how to color pictures of dogs or trees or houses. Now, we're going to color emotions. Now, let's think of an emotion. Let's pick *joy*. What color does joy feel like, what does it look like?"

Observe their choices. They'll likely think about it, and don't be surprised to find girls picking pink. They're more or less programmed to do that, but others will still pick purple or red. Red doesn't always mean anger. That in itself is a case-in-point about emotional intelligence. Emotions are complex and they are particular to those who have them. Each has to be taken in context and with full consideration for the person. A person is not the equivalent of their emotions, not even of their actions. Emotions and actions are fleeting things; people evolve over time, and a lifetime is a long time.

Watch if your kids use black to depict joy, and puzzle over that conundrum! This exercise will reflect a lot about a child's true emotions and perceptions in this way. Interpretation can be a lot of fun and can lead to great conversations that, again, allow you to connect emotionally. Don't worry about always reading a lot into some things: Why did they choose black? Should you be worried? Maybe your child is just really into Batman right now!

And don't forget to observe your own choices. What colors mean joy to you? Why? What associations do you make with that color such that it means joy to you? Understanding these things, even asking yourself the question, will create a bond between thought and emotion which we have already seen is necessary to a well-balanced psyche.

Now start coloring. Don't worry about shapes. Let the kids' instincts, and your own, decide what shapes. Perhaps you're shading it in like a sky, or you're making circles or figure eights. Just draw. It's a good idea to have some music in the background for this game, but nothing too distracting. Just enough to provide some rhythm and artistic inspiration, even subconsciously.

While coloring, ask your kids (one at a time) why they chose the color they chose, what associations they have with that color. If they don't know, that's fine too. The idea is to create the association of thought and emotion.

Pick another color/emotion and keep drawing that emotion, on the same page as the other. You can color in a different area, or right on top of the previous contribution. Use another sheet of paper if you like.

At the end, look at the results. They will likely be very abstract. Use the occasion to see what images you and your family can see in those abstract shapes and colors. This excites the imagination and continues the bond of thought and emotion. You may even be discovering hidden talents, or nurturing talents you already know are there. This principle of interpretation is one we'll come back to, like other principles we discuss in these early-age games.

Picture This, Jr. Edition:

Before playing this game, pop over to the internet and print up some pictures. It is perfectly fine to print them in black and white. Just search for free images using keywords of the various emotions you're becoming familiar with using. Make sure frustration or anger are among the emotions, but don't only include negative emotions. Print one for each emotion. Write the emotion on the back of the picture, but in pencil and small and located where only you can see it.

To play the game, sit with the pictures face down in front of you. Raise one picture and have your kids guess what emotion they're seeing. Note that they may not get it right, and that's good. For one child, frustration and anger may look quite the same. This will be quite telling. If frustration and anger are synonymous to your child, they're likely to respond to their frustration with anger (or sadness with love), and that's what emotional intelligence is meant to curb (among other things). But frustrated anger is a key sign of a lack of emotional intelligence (as is, of course, mistaking sadness and love).

Ask your children to plumb their feelings here. Why do they mistake one emotion for another, if they do? What indicates one emotion over another? Ask them to verbalize their feelings of these emotions, whatever they may be. These answers will be more sophisticated as we move on to more challenging versions meant for older kids, but this is a golden opportunity to prime your children to pursue the connection between reason and emotion, between cause and effect, and to be mindful of other people and why they feel as they do.

You won't be giving any answers in this game, so you're off the hook. But don't be afraid to challenge yourself when hearing your children's answers. Do you sympathize with their perspective? What's causing it? Is there some positive way you can influence them based on their answers, perhaps a problem stemming from your own perspective?

Toy With Me:

Here's a variation on *Picture This*, and it builds on those skills. This one is ideal to play with one child, but it's good for two or three (larger numbers get difficult with this game). This one's great for the room where children often play and where their toys are most-often stored.

Simply ask your child to introduce you to some of their toys, or to talk about them if you're already acquainted (you remember Buzz Lightyear). So, take the toy in question and ask your child what emotion they associate with the toy. Is this a happy toy, an angry toy? They're not all happy after all. Darth Vader isn't a very happy chap, nor are one or more of the Transformers characters, nor might be any array of stuffed animals.

Ask your child to explain why the characters feel as they do. The reason this is such a fun game is that the children already know the answers; they know the backstory of Boba Fett or Yoda or whatever character the toy represents. It's something they already have an interest in, and it plays to their strengths.

It also helps them understand (by verbalizing) the connection between emotion and cause. Darth Vader is angry because his beloved wife was lost years before. Godzilla is angry that he was awakened from his slumber (which may also account for his radioactive breath). One toy or another may have a backstory which your child has created. They may just make one up on the spot! That's great, it means the game is exciting their sense of narrative, that they're ready to understand another person's perspective and its associations to their emotions. That is how they'll come to see the connection between their own emotions and the things which caused them.

Something to note about most stuffed animals is that, as often as they are well-known characters like Kermit the Frog, they are often more generic. This gives children the chance to create their own narratives, probably influenced by narratives they know or narratives they are living or believe they are living. Show curiosity about the stuffed animals which don't have fixed backstories and ask your children about them. Listen closely to their answers, as they could just as easily be painting a self-portrait without knowing it.

THE APE FAMILY:

Here's a fun game for indoors or out, a large family or small. It's a playacting exercise, which you've already done with your family with *Making Faces*. But this one uses the whole body, and belongs in a bigger room like a living room or family room, not the dining table where some of these games can sometimes be played.

To play *The Ape Family*, designate roles in the family. You may be the parent of either gender, or you may choose to play a child and let a child play the adult. Many people assume the same roles in the Ape Family as they occupy in their own. That's fine, it's not the central issue.

Now go about a day in the life of a regular human family. Do cleaning chores, homework, and have dinner. The rules are, of course, that you can't use any words. You can only emote in order to get your points across.

It's harder than you think!

You might find yourself getting frustrated, emotions building. Who knows how things will turn out? Probably, you'll have to calm things down, so keep an eye on it. Of course, whenever emotions prevail and there is a distinct lack of reason, as things are in the Ape Family household, things need to be closely monitored.

That's the point.

Now, we're not trying to encourage a row with your family. There's a lot to be learned here about how to read people, how to sympathize with emotional expressions, how to better control your own frustrations and tendencies to outburst. Parents often lose track of that, and an outburst of temper can be very harmful to children. They are also commonly overlooked and commonly emulated and repeated from one generation to the next.

OUTDOORS

Stop And Toss:

Here's a good game for the backyard, and we don't recommend it for the dinner table or living room. One glance at the game's name will probably tell you everything you need to know about why!

This game works with several children or even just one! It's good for building cooperation between siblings or between parents and kids too.

Take the family out to the yard with your ball to toss. Establish a rotation, starting with you as the game leader. As the holder of ball, you can choose whom to throw it to, including yourself. Passing it to yourself means tossing it straight up, not far, and catching it again. But you must call that person (or yourself) out first. Everybody gets one choice, so if you choose yourself, the ball automatically goes to the next person in the rotation after you've done that pass to yourself. If you call out a person across from you and they choose themselves, they throw to themselves after receiving the ball from you, and then of course pass the ball to the next person in the rotation.

First, this instills thoughtfulness before action. Catching the ball is the initial response, the thought. Choosing who to throw it to represents the thought, and the toss is their action. It may also reveal, as other games have already done, which pairs in the family have the strongest bonds and which the weakest. Use your own growing emotional intelligence to decipher why that is and how you can gently influence it.

The game is as simple as that. But you can make it more challenging in the following 'second round'...

STOP AND TOSS

Game Rotation

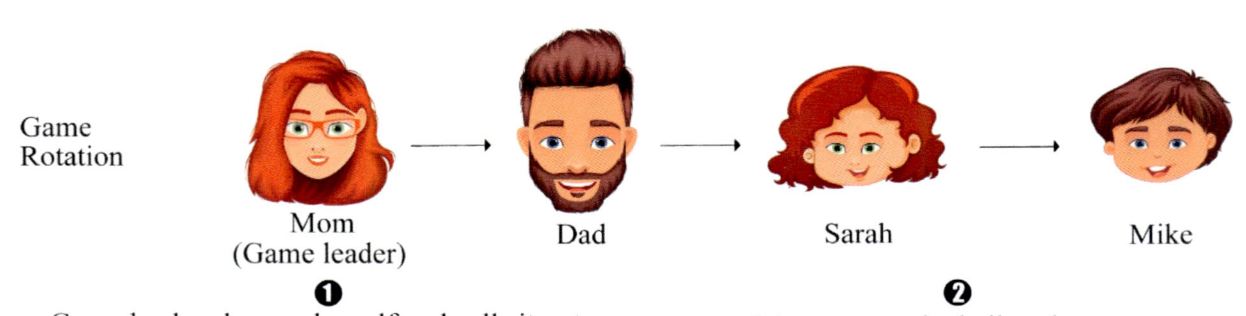

Mom (Game leader) → Dad → Sarah → Mike

❶

a. Game leader chooses herself and calls it out.

b. She tosses the ball straight up and catches it again.

❷

Mom passes the ball to the next person in the rotation - dad.

Let every holder of the ball imagine a small trick they can do with the ball, then announce it. After doing the trick, the child announces the person whom they've chosen to pass the ball to. Such easy and fun tricks include things the very young can do:

- Turn around
- Touch the ground
- Touch the top of the head
- Rub the tummy

If you're playing this with older children and younger, you'll want to let the older kids do more complicated tricks, some of which might be:

- Weaving the ball through the legs
- Looping the ball around the back
- Raising the ball over the head
- Bouncing it on top of the head
- Bouncing the ball (if the ball will bounce)

Note what tricks they choose, and what kind of physical dexterity they exhibit.

Also take note if they consistently pass it to themselves a lot, as this may reveal early signs of isolation, loneliness, or narcissistic and antisocial inclinations. It's always good to catch things early, so ask them how they are feeling that day. The game can become a useful precursor to a really important conversation.

Keep the game advancing by letting kids do two tricks before passing the ball. Encourage them to make up their own tricks. Enjoy their choices and reward them with laughter and support. Always laugh with them and never at them, of course.

Stop And Toss, Emotional Edition:

This one might be better for slightly older kids, but do allow your younger kids the chance to try. You might be surprised what they come up with! Follow the same rules for *Stop and Toss*. Only this time, instead of doing any tricks with the ball, have the kids designate an emotion to the ball, and then enact that emotion. As the game leader, you begin with an example.

Pick 'fear' and then direct fear at the ball. Toss it up and flinch, make a frightened face and shriek in fear. Be exaggerated and comical, illicit as much enthusiasm as you can. Then decide who you'll toss the ball to, and toss it. Let the next person choose their own emotion, then demonstrate it, then they pick the next person (an important detail) and pass the ball.

Note who chooses what kind of emotion. What does it reveal about their development (and this could be your or your spouse or partner as much as any of the kids)? Make sure to guide the game, adding positive emotions if they seem to be lacking. If they are, what does that indicate about the state of your family? Is there too much negative emotion in your house? Why? Who brings that into the house? You? If so, you know you have to take some positive action to change that circumstance.

To challenge your kids' memory (and your own) try combining both games. First, the child or parent catches the ball, they name an emotion and enact it, then do a trick, then choose a person to pass the ball to. Like *Simon* and so many other games, this will strengthen them intellectually while they play. It also naturally encourages the bond between emotionality and intellect, and that's central to emotional intelligence.

3a

Dad announces a trick and performs the trick.

4

a. Dad chooses Mike and announces it.
b. Dad passes the ball to Mike.

3b

Dad announces an emotion and enacts the emotion towards the ball.

If any of the players forget to do one or the other (omitting an emotion/enactment or a trick), let them skip a turn. Mistakes and mishandling of the cycle of behavior have consequences, and this is a good way to learn that. Don't be too hard on them, though. Allow them to have some positive associations with failure. It's part of the process of success, and you can remind them of that.

BACKYARD SOUP:

This is fun game for young kids, girls especially. It's great for several kids, so if your kid is having a playdate or if you have several children, try to whip up a batch of this tasty confection!

Simply decide you'll be making some backyard soup. You can prepare a list of common background items you might use, including:

- Rocks
- Pebbles
- Sticks
- Leaves
- Grass

Or you can let the child decide what ingredients you will use at your gentle prompting. Go about gathering these things, letting the children work together as much as possible. Designate an area on the grass that will be the soup pot (so you don't need to actually use one), and have them place the items in the pot. Let them set about their shared task of cooking the soup, with your participation as required.

The game should encourage cooperation and create a bond over a shared task. It should inspire their imaginations and encourage them to use those imaginations more and more, fostering an inquisitive nature. Ask them to describe what items have different effects on the soup. Do leaves make it sweeter? Do branches have vitamins? Stones are iron-rich, perhaps? Let them decide what purpose these things have, and let them be mindful that everything has a purpose. Emotions have a purpose too, and being able to recognize them is a big part of emotional intelligence.

One important thing is that their cooperation may bring about conflicts, as these things are apt to do. If that happens, note how a child's emotions and actions play out. Are they thinking before they act, as in a game of *Stop and Toss*? Are they considerate of each other's feelings as they create this soup? If not, you'll be there to gently correct them and guide them toward empathy for one another. If they are emotional when they should be reasonable, this is the time to ask them why they feel as they do, and what other things they could feel, what other things they could do. Help them resolve the conflict and go on with their shared task toward their common goal. That is the desired result of emotional intelligence, after all (one of many).

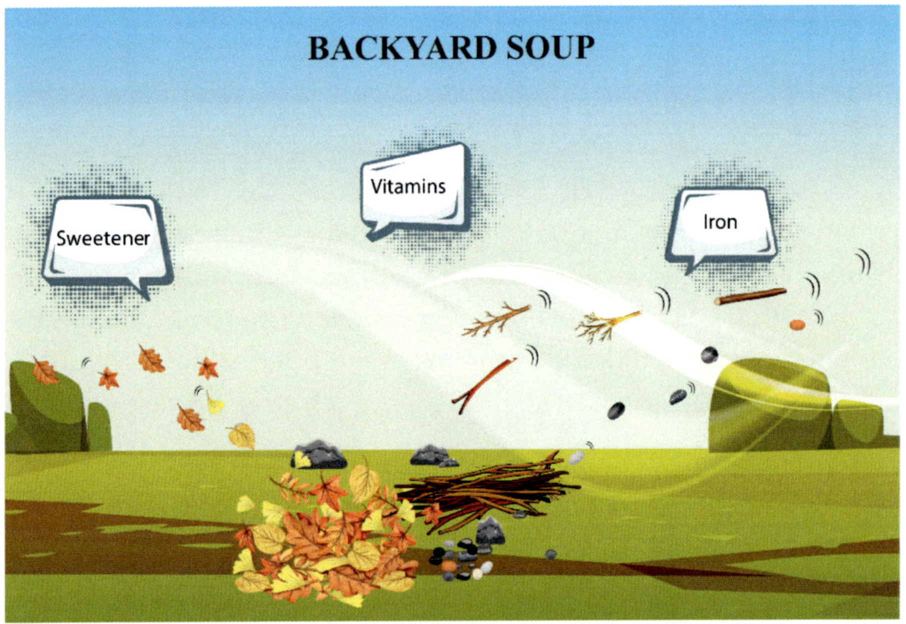

DEBRIEF

Before we move on, let's take a moment to assess. How did your young kids enjoy the games? Did they tend to get carried away? If so, do they also get carried away with their emotions outside of a game context? Did they find it hard to access their emotions during game play? How do they do with expressing emotion on a daily basis? Is there an inverse relationship, where one is actively emotional during play but otherwise recalcitrant? Is there a reverse situation? These are all red flags, as they say, things to look for, potential signs of trouble. These games are great for identifying these, and for helping to correct them. If a child is having trouble accessing or controlling their emotions, both firmly under the umbrella of emotional intelligence, these games should be repeated. Think about repeating the ones they had trouble with, or tweaking them as you feel necessary. Your particular family may require an adjustment. We don't mind.

It could be that your young child is so advanced that these games are just a piece of cake. You might try one of the games from our next chapter, filled with games for preteens. But don't rush your child either. These games are tailor-made for kids at certain developmental stages. If your child is consistently having a problem with one or more games, it could be that you've reached a developmental stumbling block.

Chapter 3

Games for Preteens (Ages 8-12)

As kids get older, they're more perceptive and more expressive, and their comprehension skills flourish. At this stage of the cycle of behavior, they are still primarily creatures of emotion, but thought becomes more important to their actions. The games in this chapter are designed to increase the demand upon interpreting emotions, and these games also start to teach the skills required for active listening.

FREAKY FRIDAY:

You may know the story trope of a body switch, often between parent and child. If you've never seen any version of this movie or its derivations, it's usually a lightning bolt or curse or something which, in this case, puts the consciousness of the child into the body of the parent and the consciousness of the parent into the body of the child. Each must live life through the other's perspective, learning empathy along the way.

Well, there's little reason you can't do this with your preteens and younger teens. Some older teens may even be willing to play along, but they're already in a strange transitional period between childhood and adulthood, so they lack the necessary physical contrast which makes this experiment impactful. Even so, they can body-swap with a younger sibling.

This is something you can do over the dinner table. A lot of these games are good for such gatherings, since that's one of the few times that you have everybody already gathered around the table. You have to talk about something other than what they learned in school that day, after all. Not that you don't want to ask that, but dinner is long.

So, try having a conversation where you're the kid and your kid is the parent. You don't have to assume a childish voice (I personally recommend against it), though your child can and probably will assume an adult voice and manner. You can affect your manner a bit, but remember that you don't want to leave your child with a lasting impression. Don't let them feel that they're being mocked or aped, or that you are. You don't want your child to see you as less than an authoritative figure in the long run, however amusing a temporary role-reversal experiment might be.

Gear the conversation toward household subjects. The idea of this experiment is to be able to see the world through somebody else's eyes, somebody whose life is comparable but different from your own. Parents and kids fit this bill perfectly.

So as the kid, ask your parent about their adult concerns. Give them a taste of what it's like in your world. Ask about things from your own work, even the stressful things. Ask them for advice for your own dealings on the schoolyard. Tease them (just a little) with some of the things they may do to annoy you. It's a great way to create empathy, to generate the ability to share a different perspective, and maybe even gently curb your children's behavior in some ways.

It may also be revealing about what kind of example you're setting. If you pay attention to their answers, you'll see their versions of you, their visions of you. Are they callous toward others when they relate stories back to the family? Do they make a lot of crude jokes? They're holding a mirror up to you. Knowing that is a huge part of your own emotional intelligence.

Be careful with this exercise. You're still the authority. If anything, this game should drive that point home. In trying to be the authority, your children should get a quick idea of how hard that can be. If you have more than one kid and they're swapping roles, don't let them mock each other overmuch. Don't let things deteriorate. You can also change roles in the middle of the game.

After the game, don't forget to discuss the game. What did the kids learn? What did you learn? Always lead by example and share first. It may take a little prodding, but digesting and understanding the lessons being learned is important. Sure, it's all fun and games, until ...

Dragon Brain:

Here's a comparable game, though it's quite a bit more complicated. The dragon, if one ever existed, would have had a brain about the size of a walnut. So gather the family wherever may be convenient and spacious, a living room or family room. It's good for outside too, and good for preteens because they're often into dragons.

Get a walnut (beforehand) and simply hand it to one family member. That person becomes a dragon. Let them go around the house as a dragon for a while, five minutes or so. Have them return to the family and return the dragon brain/walnut to the family and hand it to somebody else. How long has it been since you've had license to act like a dragon? Will you be the comical dragon from *Shrek*, or the little guy from *Doc McStuffins*, or King Ghidorah from the *Godzilla* movies?

The fun part of this role-play game is that the other family members enact the roles of the townspeople. How do they react? There's a lot of enacted emotion in this game, and no real-world conflict. It teaches kids that certain actions, friendly or unfriendly, have a direct connection to emotional reactions. The interconnectedness of these things is crucial to mastering emotional intelligence.

And speaking of monsters ...

WHAT'S MY MONSTER?:

Here's a fun combination of approaches which should appeal to older tweens. It's a great one for the dinner table. Keep your dragon brain walnut handy and pass it to the most likely player. They are to assume the character of a famous dragon. They'll know tons of them. Without saying what monster they are, have them describe themselves by characteristics. The others, contestants in the game (if you will), ask questions which will help them identify which dragon you are. Each questioner should consider the answers as clues to the solution. Let them raise their hand to be selected. It's a fun new twist on *What's My Line?* And what kid isn't a fan of that old TV show called *What's my line*? The idea here was that a person described their profession (or *line*, in the old-fashioned slang). Questioners would deduce a person's occupation through a series of questions.

Whoever guesses correctly gets to be the next dragon. Popular dragons may include:

- King Ghidorah
- Smaug
- Mushu
- Dragonite
- Toothless
- etc.

The list is frightfully long, I'm afraid. Parents may have a hard time keeping up with this game without a little internet research beforehand. Okay, here's an answer key:

- Shenron *(Dragon Ball)*
- Dragonite *(Pokemon)*

- Smaug *(The Hobbit, Lord of the Rings)*
- Viserion *(Game of Thrones)*
- Haku *(Spirited Away)*
- King Ghidorah *(Godzilla)*
- Toothless *(How to Train Your Dragon)*
- Mushu *(Mulan)*

Another rule, however, is that you cannot ask what movie or book they appeared in. It is by trait that you identify the character, by backstory. So keep the questions focused on why the dragon is the way they are, funny or in love or scary or angry. The questioning will direct the game.

TELEPHONE:

Here's a bona fide classic (a lot of these games are based on classics, which I'm sure you've noticed). This is also a superb exercise in active listening, which is a staple of emotional intelligence. Several of our games will focus on this, so this is a good one to do early on.

For those who don't know, here's how the game is played: The game leader whispers a phrase into one person's ear. Let's say, "The turtle and the hare had a race through the woods, but the hare had other things in mind." The first player, a child, repeats the sentence to the best of their ability. The second player does the same to the third, and so on. The idea is that the phrase changes from one person to the next. By the end of the line, the two phrases are compared for the divergence of the original to the final.

Good fun.

You do need a few people to do it, however. The more the merrier. Play it as you would any normal version of Telephone. For these purposes, you as the game leader may choose to include emotion references in the sentence. Then pay particular attention to how these words specifically change. You might find they become exaggerated as the sentence is passed along. Here are a few examples to get you started:

- Mary was sad that her dog ran away.
- Johnny was happy because he got a bike for his birthday.
- Peter was embarrassed when he fell on the playground.
- Dylan was proud when he won the spelling bee.

Coloring Emotions, Preteen Edition:

Kids develop artistic inclinations early, but they develop those skills as they age. So engage in the same exercise as before. But this time, instead of picking one emotion and having your kids pick their color to represent it, have them pick the emotion they'd like to draw. They're older now, capable of making that kind of choice.

So, sit there and draw your emotions. Let the colors blend, using whatever colors or strokes or styles seem appropriate. Use this time, as you did before, to talk about what emotions they chose to color and why, what things may be going on in their lives as they draw the emotions they're expressing. This is a tried-and-true method of the talking cure often called *art therapy*.

Now you've all created another abstract field, or a sky. But instead of stopping here, and instead of moving on to another emotion, you're going to draw a foreground to match the emotional background. Let everybody use black to draw the foreground, a sound artistic design. What they draw, of course, is up to them. In general, you're creating a skyscape, so your physical objects, the Earth and whatever features it offers, will be along the bottom line

of the page, occupying the bottom quarter of the page. Start from the bottom and keep it simple.

The subject in the foreground may include:

- Trees in a field
- Mountains
- A cityscape
- Houses in a suburb
- Farms
- Lonely highways
- People

What subjects the artists choose will likely reflect strongly on where their perspective is. The entire picture is likely to reveal much about where the artist's emotional head is at, if you'll pardon that expression. Is it a lonely farmhouse against a raging red sky? Is it a tranquil boat against a light-blue field? Ask your children what they're drawing and why, what feelings inspired them. Ask them if there are any narratives or stories behind the objects they're drawing. Who lives in that farmhouse? How do they feel? Why? Who is in that boat, those buildings? What are they feeling and why?

This sharpens their connections between emotions and their causes, and the place of reason amidst it all. Don't worry if neither of you can see any deeper significance in something you or they have drawn; instead, you might end up simply having a giggle about it! Any conversation with your children--deep or otherwise--is nevertheless relationship-building.

Mad Libs, Emotional Edition:

You can pick up any copy of Mad Libs or write your own. Then fill the story in with congregations of emotion words. Every noun must be an emotion, every verb, every adverb and adjective (which are often emotions anyway).

Here's an example, the insertions in italics:

Be kind to your *sadness*-footed *joys*

For a duck may be somebody's *anger*,

Be kind to your *confusion* in the *glee*

Where the weather is always *happiness*

You may think that this is the *silly*,

Well, it is.

Well, that fun little ditty certainly got heady! It's a good reminder of a few things:

- Emotions are prevalent in our lives; they're everywhere.
- Emotions are contextual, less or more intimidating when seen in different contexts.
- Emotions, often seen as adverbs or adjectives, are nouns, as concrete as any other noun.
- Emotions can be controlled and manipulated.

Emotional Ballet:

Here's another fun physical exercise, and it's much more popular among girls. It's certainly more effective among younger participants. Play some classical music suitable to ballet and pick a narrative. All ballets tell stories, after all. Here are a few classic storylines you might choose from:

- A young person (or two) wanders into the woods, meets up with a witch, and flees back to his or her home.
- A young person (or two) climbs a great beanstalk to a dangerous realm where peril and riches await.
- A young person (or two) has to cross a mighty river.

With the exception of the last one, you no doubt recognize these plotlines. Your kids will too. That will increase their confidence and willingness to participate. Of course, the rule is that they can't speak, but they must dance their roles through the story. Luckily, because the stories are so well-known, you likely won't need any narration. But you can use one if you like if you designate the narrator beforehand.

Now let 'em dance. There's something about dancing, especially for kids, that is freeing. It is for adults too, and in a similar way. People tend to lose themselves in dance, and this carries across a variety of cultures and epochs. So they'll be able to access their emotions and to express them, even if they are acted, with new and intriguing ease. How will your child enact their meeting with the witch in dance? Who will play the witch and how will they enact that?

The game further solidifies the bond between emotion and narrative, which is crucial to understanding other people's perspectives. If you vary the roles, putting the kids in the role of the adults, you may come up with some hilarious results, but keep in mind that it's really all about the kids. Your performances are meant to encourage, not eclipse.

Also, what could be more fun than dancing around with your family? And you could become a more whole family, which is our shared goal. This is where the games are at their peak, in fact. Families have altogether too little time to share and create memories like these. And both you and your family are sure to remember this exercise and many of the others.

The Screaming Pillow:

This is great for slightly younger preteens. But they'll all go along if you give them a good example. Anyway, pick up a cheap pillow and set it aside for this little game. Once you have everybody together (or you can do this one-on-one), have any player pick something they want to scream about, something which angers or upsets them, and have them scream it into the pillow. Make sure they hold it tight to dampen their scream, and then let them scream it off their chest. This can be inhibiting, so you'll want to start off and set a good example. Go ahead and scream your scream into the pillow. It's liberating and stress relieving. It feels odd at first, but it feels great afterward. It's a well-known technique in psychiatry. It also reminds everybody in the family of their commonality. Everybody has these frustrations; everybody has things which upset them. But if they just express them, without words or deeds, just empty emotion into an empty expression, it can alleviate tensions and unspent energies.

The Punching Pillow:

No doubt you already see where this is going. Let your whole family get out their built-up emotional energy by punching the punching pillow (you can let the screaming pillow do double-duty). With this game, a parent may hold the pillow for a child, or for another adult, but it's recommended to put the pillow on a big easy chair or a loveseat or sofa. Putting the punching pillow on one's lap is also effective and safe. Watch out for older kids with this game, as they may not know their own strength or the depth of their own emotions. As always, err on the side of caution. Don't let things get out of hand. As the game leader, that's up to you. The idea is to release bottled-up emotions, of which anger is the most common. The idea is not to create a temper tantrum or trigger an emotional outburst.

DEBRIEF

Before moving on, let's take a minute to digest what we've done so far. These games for preteens build on the concepts we used in games for young kids. They also build on familiar concepts which are tailored to our psychological needs. Did any of it surprise you?

What did you learn about your kids? Do they have artistic instincts and talents you didn't know about? They may only be appearing now. Did they face frustrations which caused them to react emotionally? That's a teachable moment, and a place where you may want to shift your focus. Did they meet these challenges with perfect aplomb? How about you? Did you get skunked by your kids in any of these games? (Not even *Dragon Brain?)* Losing well is a great teachable moment for your kids ... and for yourself. Hey, how often do you play a game, much less lose one, much *much* less lose one to a kid? It's got to be refreshing not to have to achieve for once.

How are they doing with these games, which are also basic exercises in challenging interaction? A whole generation of kids seemed raised to avoid competition, and these games are not stressfully competitive and much more cooperative. But it's important for anybody's emotional intelligence to be challenged and to rise to those challenges. The games will become more challenging as life becomes more challenging; both happen as life goes on and kids get older.

But kids don't all mature at the same rate. And there is a distinct overlap between teens and preteens. They often occupy the same households, and there's a particular need for such activities. It's one of the main reasons this book exists, after all!

That brings us to our next chapter, games for preteens and teens.

Chapter 4

Games for Preteens and Teens (Ages 8-18)

Children develop at different rates, and some practices can be tweaked and tailored for kids of different ages. So we're setting aside this special chapter for games that have some crossover appeal from one group to another.

Emotional Pictionary:

If your preteens are especially quick on the draw (so to speak), then this is a great family exercise. It's played just like normal Pictionary, but the answers are all emotions. Pictionary, for those who don't know, is like Charades, but with drawings instead of actions. For preteens, this might include an easier set of rules which includes facial expressions. This is actually a little harder than it sounds. How would *you* draw frustration? After happy and sad, all facial expressions look alike. But older kids should be dissuaded from using facial expressions. The reasons for this are important to understanding emotional intelligence.

Emotions manifest themselves in more ways than just facial expressions. If you want to teach your kids (and remind yourself) how to properly read people and to understand the connections between emotions and their causes, encourage them to draw anything other than facial expressions. And they don't have to be great artists either. A stick figure of slouched posture shuffling along could be tired, depressed, sad. Tears coming out of the head could denote sadness as opposed to tiredness. A stick figure jumping for joy could denote joy.

But how do you draw loneliness? One figure isolated from a crowd? How would you draw anger without drawing a facial expression? Fear?

This is a great game for lots of reasons. Like all of the games in this chapter, it can bring kids of different ages together. This is a significant problem in many households, as older kids tend to reject younger kids, just as younger kids seek the influence and approval of older kids. This game is also familiar, which is a big plus. It involves drawing, which is fun, and instant participation and gratification.

RIDDLES:

True, this isn't exactly *a* game. But riddles do have a lot we can glean from in our quest to master emotional intelligence. Primarily, they test our intelligence. But they do also test our patience, our temperament, and our egos. Some people may feel frustrated, and others foolish or tricked.

But there's more to riddles than that. There's a curious ratio with riddles. The longer they go unsolved, the more intellectual ability falters. The mind tends to circle around and around in the wrong direction, following blind alleys, getting hopelessly lost on red herrings while missing the answer, which is almost always built into the phrasing of the riddle itself. The answer is often based on synonyms.

In any case, as the mind's ability to find the answer goes on, emotion tends to increase and overtake the psyche. The more frustrated the ability to reason, the more emotion dominates. The ratio is a brutal case in point of emotional intelligence. When reason recedes, emotions will proceed. One must remain diligent about this balance.

It brings up the notion of triggers. Anybody will become more emotional as they become less rational, as the principle of the riddle proves. So one can call a riddle a trigger of these circumstances. An emotionally intelligent person knows that going into this situation, they're likely to be triggered to emotional overload. So they should be on their guard. If this is a problem for them, they should ... no, they *must*... alter the situation in some proactive way. This is a huge part of emotional intelligence and any skill set, and that is to take action to change the results once problems have been identified. It's not enough just to shrug it off as human nature because it's not human behavior, it's *a* human behavior. Behavior, as we've seen, is action. Action is entirely the province and the personal responsibility of the individual.

So a person who gets frustrated by riddles can take this as an opportunity to look for ways to change the outcome. If walking by the bakery triggers your hunger and you're trying to diet, walk a different route. Don't just bemoan the location of the bakery and keep eating.

Emotionally, if you know you can't control yourself (and part of emotional intelligence is to understand your emotions), then you should proactively avoid the challenge. It seems like a simple answer, but abstinence is a lot harder than it looks, and that's just over a simple riddle.

Imagine the challenge a person faces knowing they're likely to get into a heated argument over politics (not a game we recommend in this book). They know they'll be in the company of somebody with an opposing point of view, perhaps, or they know from experience that such conversations tend to end badly and (probably) emotionally. It's part of this person's emotional intelligence not only to recognize the danger but to prevent it. They should either determine not to bring it up, to bring up other things instead, to leave the room if the subject can't be avoided, perhaps to leave the gathering or even to abstain from going. There are a lot of alternatives to shrugging and marching headfirst into a social disaster. It's a hard lesson to teach and an even harder lesson to learn, and this is a fun way to do it.

Picture The Differences:

This one is good for a wide span of kids because the popular game can be challenging for kids of all ages, even adults. You've seen these visual comparisons, where two nearly identical pictures are set side by side and the viewer is asked to find the differences, either a certain amount of or as many as possible. The latter works well if you have older kids, who may enjoy the sense of competitiveness.

This exercise does have a lot more to do with visual and mental focus and not on emotion, though the same principle of the riddle does apply. It sharpens the eye for detail, which any person will need for strong emotional intelligence. It's the eye for detail which allows one person to understand what another person needs, on both intellectual and emotional levels.

Also, one may become frustrated over that last missing object. You might consider adding a ticking clock to the game to ramp up the pressure. Egg timers or sand timers work great for this, but your smartphone probably has a stopwatch app. If not, you can download one in seconds for free.

Now let's add another emotional element. These pictures are usually scenes including people (which makes sense in a lot of ways). Think about having your kids create a narrative for the human characters in the scene. Whether it's a picture of people in a park, people eating in a restaurant, people at the beach, there can be stories to tell.

Work something out before the comparisons begin, during, or after. But let every participant share their narrative at the end of the exercise. If they found a missing fork in one rendering of the restaurant, that can figure in. If the picture of the park featured a dog with or without a leash, that could become part of the story. As you might imagine, let the narrative evolve around some emotion, and let the object figure into the narrative. Take a picture of a restaurant, for example:

Menu
Menu

The man at the counter is sitting with his back to the two women sitting at the table because they had a fight. But he didn't have a napkin or a third meatball, and that made him even more frustrated. Even worse, the coatrack only has two prongs instead of three, reminding him that he hasn't seen his two best friends in a long time.

It's pretty easy to cook up a narrative like this. It won't win any prizes, but it does a lot to establish and reaffirm the connections between emotions and events and the practice of empathy for the perspectives of others.

Pay attention to the answers, as they will reveal a lot about what the person answering may feel about themselves and their place in the world around them. This may alert you to any potential problems in the making.

Make sure to be generous with your praise for their efforts. Even participating could be an improvement! And that encourages further participation.

Simon:

By now you've recognized some classic games at the root of our exercises, and there's good reason for that. These games are based on developmental fundamentals, ours and theirs. We all drink from the same water, as it were. And the rules of some of these games are well-known, and that makes them easy to play and effective as teaching moments.

Also, the publishers want to say we're not in the business of promoting and selling toys. We don't take any money in sponsorship, and we're not associated with Hasbro or any other entity.

That said, this time we're going straight to the source. *Simon* is a simple memory game. It has a wide age-range of players and is easy to learn. The plastic colorful nodules of the Simon device light up (and each emit their own sound) in a repeating sequence which gets longer by one with each rotation. The job is to remember the sequence and repeat it back. The longer the sequence, the more challenging. The game can play faster for older or more advanced players.

This game is predicated on the same principles of active listening. The player engages in a lot of the same activities, including focus and repeating back inputted information.

It has an emotional aspect as well, as cold as it seems. The game becomes progressively more difficult and that happens relatively quickly. As we've done so many times, while your child focuses on the game, you are focusing on your child. How are they reacting to the increasing stress and pressure? How are they dealing with the other players (if there are any, as you can play this game alone) who are watching, not only as onlookers but as competitors? Are they taunting the player, or are they demonstrating emotional intelligence? Perhaps taunting him is a sign of emotional intelligence. EI is about understanding what causes emotions in other people as well as themselves, also how to prepare for, manage, avoid, or deter negative conditions and their results. It's not merely synonymous with being nice. So, in the same way members of one baseball team try to psych out the batter of the other team, which shows a high-level understanding of emotional intelligence, so too could any taunting. But this can have drastic and dramatic results on the player, especially if they are emotionally vulnerable or volatile.

In any case, high performance at this particular game indicates intelligence, a willingness to fail and try again, and active listening.

I Went To Market

A similar game is played like this:

- A player takes a can and says, "I went to market, bought a fat pig, and this."
- They hand the can to the next player, who repeats the previous item and adds their own before handing the can along: "I went to market, bought a fat pig, *a hairy goat*, and this."
- They hand it to player number three, who repeats the first two items, in order, adds their own, and passes it down the line.

It's a good memory game for the whole family, and an increasingly challenging memory game.

Wipeboard Brainstorming:

Again, not a single particular game. Really, we're talking about brainstorming using a wipe board. But ... brainstorming what?

Emotions, of course.

You're the game leader, so put yourself at the board and make five columns with four vertical lines. Leave a space at the top and write in that space: *what*, *where*, *when*, *why*, *how*. You may want to print up emotions on a piece of paper and precut them to fill a jar or the bowl or hat. Let the kids pick a piece of paper to choose the emotion. Let's say the emotion is *confusion*, that goes in the *what* column, the first column.

Next is where, and this is where the brainstorming begins. Where does confusion happen? Have your family shout out their answers to keep things fun. You may have to sift through the answers, or you may establish a hand-raising rule, whatever works for you.

So, where does confusion happen?

- A new place
- Math class
- A riddle
- Church
- On a date
- In a play
- In a test center
- In a dream

And so on. When can confusion occur?

- In the middle of the night
- First thing in the morning
- After a fight or argument

WIPEBOARD BRAINSTORMING

What	Where	When	Why	How
Confusion	A new place	In the middle of the night		
	Math class	First thing in the morning		
	A riddle	After a fight or argument		
	Church	During the holidays		
	On a date	When you're in love		
	In a play	When you're emotional		
	In a test center	When communication breaks down		
	In a dream	When somebody needs a favor		
		When you need a favor		

- During the holidays
- When you're in love
- When you're emotional
- When communication breaks down
- When somebody needs a favor
- When you need a favor

Don't discount the last two; those can be tremendously confusing and conflicting situations.

Let your family spitball things with you writing down the answers. Once the whole board is full, you've excited their minds about understanding the causes, the triggers, of these emotions and, thereafter, ensuing behaviors. Talk about them, consider them. Are they the triggers which occur in their lives? Most likely, that's the case. And that can clue you into ways to gently correct those problematic perspectives before they become problematic behaviors.

Emotional Improvisation:

Here's a fun game for older or advanced preteens, and teens of all ages. It's a basic role play game (at the heart of improvisation). In traditional improv (as it's called), participants are given a person, a place and an occupation to enact. Some examples might be:

- A policeman walks into a pet shop
- Santa Claus gets stranded on the side of the road
- An evangelist preacher fights a speeding ticket in court
- A pregnant woman climbs Mt. Everest
- A therapist waits in line at a New York deli
- Two fruit flies meet in a New York deli

The rules of improv are that you can't say no and you have to accept the premise. And these rules all hold for our version, only now we're going to include emotions:

- An angry dentist visits the IRS
- A confused man wanders through an amusement park
- An impatient woman goes into a library

That's pretty much all you need to know. These little scenes won't go on for too long, about three minutes or so. So you, as the game leader, will make sure to cut them off when necessary. Mix up the players to create different chemistry and to keep people in the game. Afterward, discuss it. You probably won't have learned any great lessons, but you will almost certainly be able to remark on the cleverness and inventiveness of the participants. And you may just be fostering hidden comedic or acting skills. Improv has a lot to teach budding writers and directors as well.

Spinning Wheel:

This one's great for a big crowd, and it's best for a yard or public park. Put a parent in the center, the father probably, then the mother on one side, eldest child on the other, with the kids getting progressively smaller as they reach out toward the ends. Have the kids on one side face one way, kids on the other face the other way so that nobody is running backwards. This way, everybody is running forwards, holding hands. Now start spinning. You may start going progressively faster until somebody loses their grip. Obviously, you have to be aware of the child's safety.

Still, this is a great game for a number of reasons. It instills family bonding, the importance of family connection. It instills empathy, because neither the person on the outside nor the person on the inside of any clasp wants the outside person to fall away. They are locked together against the outside forces of speed and momentum and g-forces. They have a common goal.

Not only that, but this particular game, unlike a lot of the others (not necessarily to their benefit) entails speed. It moves fast; it's a rush. It requires running and engaging physical activity. It has a rollercoaster-type thrill for younger kids, and that will instill in them a love of family gameplay later. Be careful with kids who are too young, however, lest they be accidentally hurt.

Three-Legged Races:

As long as you're already outside, try some three-legged races. Bring a few rags or scarves or even an Ace bandage and bind the legs of two runners together, then stage a few races. This one takes at least four people, as you may imagine. The benefits are more than just a fun day at the park. Competition will lead to defeat, and learning defeat is crucial to developing emotional intelligence (just ask the generation who all won participation trophies). It is more than just a race game, as it also features a true physical closeness which is sometimes lacking in families, Like *Huggy Jail*, this is a time to get close and create memories which will last a lifetime. It's also important not to let your kids grow up with too little intimacy, as it can contribute to feelings of isolation and lead to a maladjusted and lonely adulthood.

A fun variation of this game is to have the parents carry their children instead of being strapped to them, though this version does entail a risk of injury from falling. Helmets and other sensible safety precautions are recommended.

MAKING A MATCH:

Here's a good wipe board exercise. It's great for kids of various ages because each can answer according to their own current development.

Draw a line across the top to allow room to write above, then vertical lines to create five columns. Label the columns *happy, sad, mad, confused, afraid.*

Now simply ask the kids, by raising of a hand or your selection, to select a character for a column. Start with the *happy* column. What are some happy characters?

- Bugs Bunny
- Mickey Mouse
- Bilbo Baggins
- Woody the Cowboy
- Dash Incredible
- Ace Ventura, Pet Detective
- Han Solo
- Try a few for the *sad* column:
- Eeyore the Donkey
- Rapunzel
- Hamlet
- Geppetto
- Cinderella
- Bruce Wayne/Batman
- Need a few characters you'd call *afraid*?
- C3-PO
- Jar Jar Binks
- Martin Brody (Jaws)
- Scooby Doo
- Lou Costello

And so on. Your kids will know a ton of characters from shows they watch to fill in these columns. Talk to them about who these characters are and why they feel that way. They'll be happy to explain. Let's take a look at all the good this exercise can do.

It naturally strengthens the connection between emotions and characters and circumstances. Hamlet isn't just moody; after all, his father was murdered and he suspects his mother's new husband. Olive Oil isn't fearful and weird for no reason; she's constantly imperiled.

It also excites the kids' sense of narrative, which they'll use for so many applications. It strengthens bonds among the family as each learns from the other. It's not just you telling them about Martin Brody's fear of the water, but them telling you about how Anakin Skywalker became Darth Vader.

This demonstrates an interest in their world, a shared interest into the things they're interested in. That will generate mutual admiration and respect. This works between siblings too. They'll learn about the traditions of storytelling, and gain insight into the others' world.

It's also a good way to keep tabs on what your kid is watching, listening to, or reading in a way which is fun and interactive, much more so than actually watching a *Star Wars* movie.

Making A Match

HAPPY	SAD	MAD	CONFUSED	AFRAID
Bugs Bunny	Eeyore the Donkey			C3-PO
MickeyMouse	Rapunzel			Jar Jar Binks
Bilbo Baggins	Hamlet			Martin Brody (Jaws)
Woody the Cowboy	Geppetto			Scooby Doo
Dash Incredible	Cinderella			Lou Costello
Ace Ventura, Pet Detective	Bruce Wayne /Batman			
Han Solo				

Emotional Titles:

Here's another fun group activity, and fun for the wipe board. Make four columns and list them *movies, TV, books, songs.* Now you're looking for titles in any category which have an emotion in the title. Your kids will know a lot of them, especially in the songs category. Here are some examples:

- Thin Line Between Love and Hate
- Do You Love Me?
- Love Me Tender
- Land of Confusion
- Dazed and Confused
- State of Confusion
- Love Actually
- Joy Ride
- The Joy Luck Club
- Love, American Style
- Everybody Loves Raymond
- Anger Management
- Mad About You
- Bitter
- Love You Madly
- Angry
- Fear the Walking Dead
- Fear and Loathing in Las Vegas
- I Just Want You to Hurt Like I Do
- Jealous Guy
- Love Letters

As you generally should, discuss the answers. Did your teenage son recommend Hunter S. Thompson's drug-addled comic tome set in Nevada? What music are your kids listening to? If the titles have a lot of dark language, such as you might find in death metal songs (*I Am Hated, I Hate Everything About You*), it might give you reason to look into what they're listening to and why. What is it inside them which these songs express? All these exercises are great ways to get to know your kids better, and a chance for them to get to know you better too.

You can also use this game, and some others, as a chance to enlighten kids as to stories, characters, books and movies and other cultural influences that they wouldn't come to know otherwise. That's a big part of being a good parent and preparing them for the world that awaits them.

Emotional Crosswords:

This one is great for vocabulary (as you can imagine), understanding how relationships work with one another, and it helps reduce emotions to something which is easy to handle, simple words on a page.

It's not exactly the classic game, but the roots are the same. Give every participant a piece of paper and have them write a word across the middle. The word can be any emotion or trait of reasonable length. Or it can be a thought word of reasonable length. *Joy* doesn't work as well as *relief* because the latter has more letters. In any case, have the participants think of related words which share one of those letters. They can be related in just about any way, as opposites or synonyms, related circumstances or causes. Put the main word in all caps and let the related words go vertically in lowercase for easy reading.

Unlike the original, how incidental letters relate to one another doesn't really matter. Synonyms are good learning tools, but opposites are good, too. You can do this one on the wipe board, and you can use an egg timer to add that ticking clock which always adds suspense and drama.

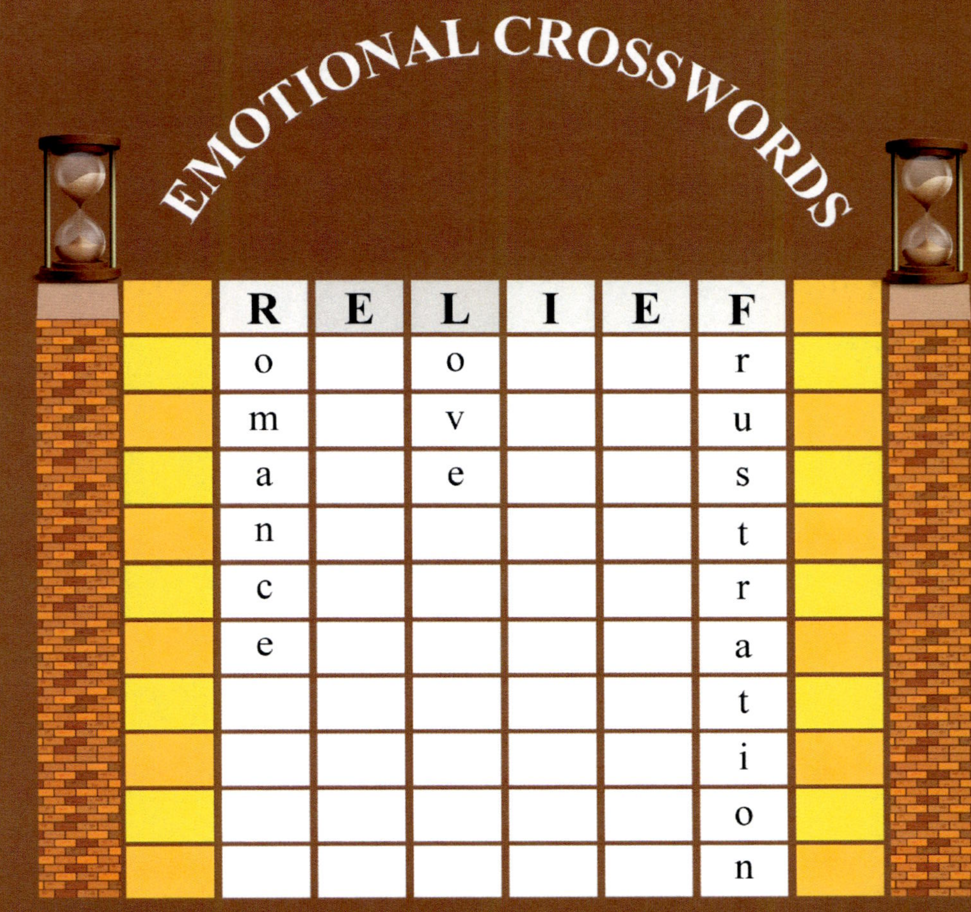
EMOTIONAL CROSSWORDS
RELIEF
Romance
Love
Frustration

EMOTIONAL TIC-TAC-TOE:

Here's another spin on a classic game that every kid knows, with enough intellectual challenge to keep older kids engaged.

First of all, instead of X's and O's, the players are Emotions and Thoughts. We've looked into the crucial differences between them, and how important it is for thoughts to govern emotions in their balance. You may take a little time to prepare for this, printing cards which read either Emotions or Thoughts. Put nine on a sheet and cut them into pieces. On another piece of card stock, print the famous Tic-Tac-Toe grid.

Now have the participants play the game as usual, but here's the twist. When the *emotion*s player lays down a card, they must utter an emotion (confusion, joy, worry, curiosity, anger, whatever). The *thoughts* player lays down their card and offers a thought which is contrary to the emotion. For example:

- Emotion: Fear
- Thought: Reassurance

- Emotion: Anger
- Thought: Forgiveness

- Emotion: Joy
- Thought: Caution

And don't worry about running out of combinations. There can be several counters to any emotion:

- Emotion: Fear
- Thoughts: Reassurance, information, odds, faith

It's true that the person with the emotions cards have less to play with, as it were. But they're learning from the thoughts, likely more numerous, even while they're playing the emotions cards. The lesson gets through just the same.

That's about all there is to it! Have fun with this one and your preteens and your teens. It's a good one for them to play unsupervised, too!

Fear	Reassurance	Comfort
Forgiveness	Anger	Relief
Caution	Joy	Sadness

Making Introductory Speeches:

This is a great pseudo-role play game that's great for developing a number of emotional intelligence facets. It's great for siblings, but only children can participate with their friends or with you. The game is to pretend you're introducing another person to a big crowd who does not know that person. The trick is to describe them by traits. For this version of the game (there's a second version for older teens exclusively), make sure only good qualities are included. Have them begin with something like, "Ladies and gentlemen, it's my pleasure to introduce my brother ..." Then go ahead and list their good points before announcing them by name. The others give them a warm welcoming applause.

This is a great game for discovering and acknowledging the qualities of another person. This is crucial to emotional intelligence, and also to empathy, part of all the higher skill sets. It provides an immense sense of being accepted and loved and fills the participants with self-esteem. It associates thoughts with emotions, demonstrating that speaking well of somebody can fill them with positive emotions, and the opposite is also true.

Sing The Family Blues:

This is a great one for kids old enough to think fast and young enough not to feel self-conscious. Everybody knows the blues, that familiar shuffling rhythm and chord progression. It's so well known, in fact, that almost anybody can try to whip up a blues song on the spot.

Start with a steady clapping rhythm (on every other beat, starting on the second one, so that you're clapping on the even-number beats). Then start singing, one person at a time in a specified rotation.

And that's just what you'll all be doing. We suggest you make the chorus steady and repetitive so that the singers can concentrate on improvising the verses. Here's a little example for a first, introductory verse:

My name is Adrienne, my children call me Mom
I'll tell you who I am and I'll tell you where I'm from
I got the blues, oh yes, I got the blues
My family is here, let me make it clear
I'll sing the family blues ...

Now just switch out the first two lines:

My real first name is Mike, my kids, they call me Dad
You know I gave my family everything I had ...

Or:

I'm the oldest son, I like to play football
I send 'em on the run, but I'm only three feet tall!

Or:

I like to go to school, and play in the park
Even though my name isn't Robert or Mark

Or:

I love my kitty cat, her name is Mrs. Meow
She likes to play with yarn, yes she does, and how!

You get the idea. The age of the kids is pretty crucial here. Coming up with rhymes like that isn't easy. A good clue is that they can put their verse together while the others are singing their verses, so they don't have to be top-level improvisers. Still, it takes a quick mind with some level of maturity. My niece of twelve years can do it, but her kid sister of about ten has trouble. Beginners can create a gap fill sheet with starting phrases and gaps to finish off the lines, which would indicate the lengths of lines needed, rhymes required, etc., making lyric writing more manageable.

What's My Emotion?

This game is based on the classic game show, *What's My Line*? (Don't be surprised if you haven't heard of it; it's *that* classic.) Contestants ask questions of a mystery guest to deduce their occupation. In this case, the guest is an emotion. Pick one family member to play the emotion and the others will ask questions. Give the participants paper and pen so they can list the questions and answers the others ask to try to solve the identity. It's like the wipe board trigger game, but better for older preteens or younger teens. Some example questions may include:

- Where do you happen?
- When are you found most?
- When are you found least?
- Do I want you or not?
- Do you happen all the time?

Questions like this will not only reveal the identity of the emotion in question; they will reveal a lot about the person asking them, especially as regards to frequency. And the kids who answer the fastest may have the most affinity to that emotion, whatever it may be. That can give you further clues as to any budding maladjustment which may be going on.

Self-Portrait

This is a great way for older tweens and younger teenagers to take art therapy to another level. The tradition of the self-portrait is long and illustrious. Fun fact, the earliest known art, cave paintings, are basically self-portraits, in wide-angle shots. Leonardo di Vinci, Vincent van Gogh, and many greats have done self-portraits.

Allow your children any colors or medium they prefer. Give them time to do it (you should be doing your own). Note how they represent themselves, as there is hardly a more autobiographical thing than a self-portrait. This will reveal not only how they see themselves physically, which should be very revealing, but how they see themselves emotionally and how they feel about themselves emotionally. This is more important than you might think. It's at this age that reverse body dysmorphia often sets in. This is a severely distorted view of one's appearance, often leaning toward the grotesque. In this view, the traits which are perceived as negative are exaggerated and the traits which are perceived as positive are forgotten. It's a crippling perspective which can inhibit all manner of positive social development. A self-portrait at this vulnerable age will reveal any possible reverse dysmorphia which may be developing and give you a chance to gently correct it before it becomes a problem. It's extremely common and does not have to become debilitating if it is caught early and dealt with properly. And that can be as simple as sharing your own tales of reverse body dysmorphia (if you have some) and how you overcame it (if you did).

Also, a self-portrait is one of those keepsakes you'll keep forever.

An intriguing counter to the self-portrait is the dual portrait. This requires two or more people. If you only have one child, you can be the other participant. If you have two kids, they paint each other. Three or more can paint in a sort of circle, everybody painting either the person to their left or right, or sitting directly across from them.

That depends on how many people you have, how much room you have, and what configuration the participants are in.

Now have them do their portraits. Encourage them to paint what they're seeing, the person drawing them, (or drawing somebody else as the case may be) or it can be an abstract or a portrait out of context. Drawing a person is especially interesting because of the general focus and direction such an expression is likely to have. That may be more likely tackled by older teens rather than younger. And remember, it's a social experiment and not an art class.

The benefits of this exercise are unique and varied. Here, the artist is forced to focus on the subject and study what is behind the appearance. They may be drawing the person, but very often portraits reveal the temperament of the person, so a natural narrative may arise. Take a look at the faces of van Gogh's peasants or the characters in Picasso's blue period. What life stories do those wizened, saddened expressions hide? What do they reveal?

And if the two artists are siblings (or family members of any sort really), the practice forces the participants to see their subject in a new light, a new context. Drawing somebody's portrait naturally generates a shared perspective, empathy for the subject in the artist just as the artist hopes to generate empathy in the viewer. This practice thereby instills empathy among family members, and that's crucial to establishing and maintaining a whole family.

And if you think a self-portrait looks cute on the wall, wait until you have a pair of portraits, each drawing the other. And if it's good enough for Vincent and Gaugin, it's good enough for any of us!

EMOTIONAL SCAVENGER HUNT:

This one's great for kids in this middle-age range. It's a great activity for siblings of these ages. Older preteens are smart enough to solve the riddles, while younger teens are still whimsical enough to get into it. But it takes some planning on your part.

What you're doing basically is providing a puzzle which, when solved, leads the participant to the answer to the riddle. Pieces of the puzzle are associated with clues to the location of the next piece. For example:

- First clue: Needles and pins, needles and pins
- First guess: Your sewing kit (if you have one and they know it)
- Second guess: Pine logs near the fire place
- Third guess: A souvenir from your family trip to Needles, Arizona

You get the idea. Your kid or kids can work together or compete to find the clue hidden in one of those locations. Let's say they find the clue. It will be a physical object with a printed clue to the next location. The objects may appear random: a button, a set of keys, or whatever. Once they find the last clue, it will be accompanied by a small piece of paper with, "Now solve the riddle!"

The items of the riddle will reveal the emotion you're looking for. If the emotion was confusion, you have left a coin, a fuse, and picture of your son or daughter, or of our solar system's sun.

Coin + fuse + son = confusion.

There are other ways to do it. The clues can be pictures which put together a story. The first picture may be a man, the second a woman, the third a heart, and the fourth a broken heart. What is the emotion they were hunting? Sadness. The clues are simply to lead them to the location of the clues. *Eat, sleep, and be merry* could direct them to the fridge, pantry, bed, bedroom, or Christmas tree. *Think you know it all?* may lead them to the family study and after that, the dictionary. Don't make it too hard or too easy. You can always give them hints if they need it. You're participating only as the game leader, since you set the clues and already know the solution. Don't let the kids get stumped for too long; that's not what this exercise is about.

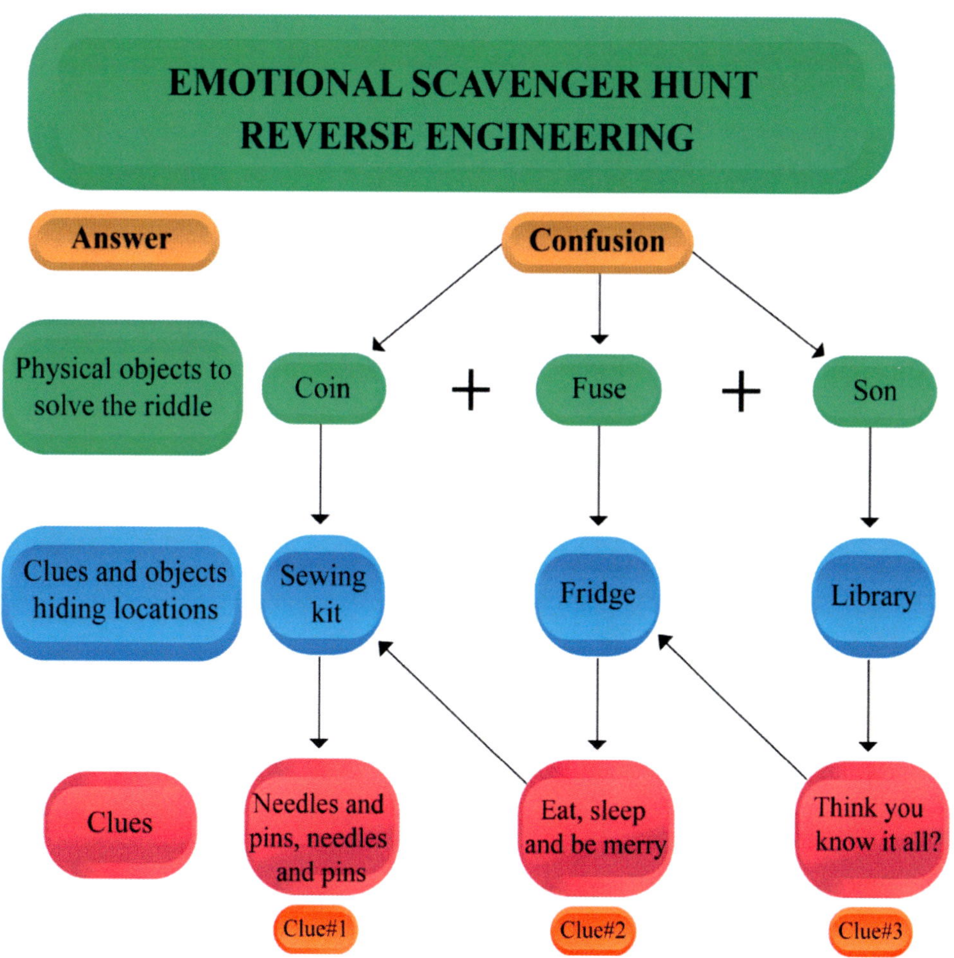

You'll be creating bonds between the participants as they work together toward a shared goal. They are also bound to foster a greater appreciation for the other's skills. If you make it competitive, each will get a point for who solves the next location and for who solves the riddle. Call it two points per clue and five points for the final answer. But older kids competing with younger kids can get a bit one-sided, so take that into consideration.

We suggest you reverse-engineer the game. Start with the solution to the puzzle and work backwards to assemble the clues. Then write, print, and cut the clues into smaller pieces of paper. Tape them to the clues and hide them the day before. You may even do the game three times, with three sets of clues and three solutions. It's a bit of prep, but it's really worth it. You're certain to delight and challenge them, all the while increasing their emotional intelligence.

CRIMEBUSTERS:

Somewhere between *Emotional Scavenger Hunt* and *What's My Emotion?* there is *Crimebusters*. In this game, your kids are detectives and you, your spouse or partner, or both, are the witnesses. The culprit, in this case, is an emotion. Give them each a tablet (or folded piece of paper) and a pencil or pen.

You start by saying something like, "Detective, I saw who it was."

They ask, "Can you describe the culprit?"

You shake your head. They ask you questions to describe the emotion. Questions they might ask can include:

- What did the culprit look like?
- What did the culprit sound like?
- What did the culprit do?
- Where did the culprit go?
- Was the culprit laughing?
- Was the culprit crying?

You can always lead with suggestions if they're not coming up with them.

- I think it was smiling
- I think it was laughing
- I think it was also crying
- And so on.

It's got a bit more pop than the *20 questions* version, as it has role play and a fictive criminal element. Kids do still love playing cops and robbers, after all.

Emotional Obstacle Course:

This originates as a psychological experiment in communications skills. And those skills certainly come into play here, though our focus is once again on trust, empathy, social interaction, and developing family bonds, things which you will have noticed are at the core of all our games in this book.

In this game's original incarnation (and you may want to try this in your own office space, along with a lot of these exercises), an office space might be rearranged to create an obstacle course. One person is blindfolded and brought to the beginning of the course. It's important that they haven't seen the course before starting it or it will be imprinted in their memory. Either one other person or more call out directions to that person to get through the maze without touching (or even glancing at) any of the obstacles. You can see where clear communications skills come into play.

In this case, you probably don't want to move the furniture of your house around. So we'll take a different approach. Choose a big area, like the front or back yard if you have one. You may need to clear some space otherwise. But we'll be doing this in negative space. Instead of avoiding obstacles, the person will walk toward an obstacle and stop short, in the case a chair. Direct the person toward the chair without passing it or hitting it. Then direct them to turn and proceed to the next chair. It's an easier way of affecting the same result. As in the other version, make sure the player doesn't see the arrangement of the chairs before beginning the course.

As mentioned at the beginning of this game, this exercise is great for building trust and family bonds. The blindfolded person is relying on the director to get them through the course. And empathy is generated on the director's part as they try to get the blindfolded player through. It's fun, and it doesn't require too much prep. You can also change the course easily simply by moving the chairs. Of course, make sure the next participant doesn't set eyes on the new course before beginning it.

DEBRIEF

What did you garner from these games? Did you notice a bonding between children of differing (but comparable) age groups? Did the younger rise to the behavior of the older, or was the reverse the case? Was the older tolerant of the younger? What did you learn from the portraits? How do your children see you, your spouses, or themselves?

It's all food for thought, to be sure. But we're not finished eating yet. Now that the kiddies have left the table, it's time for the adults (and near-adults) to get down to the most sophisticated exercises we have: games for teenagers.

Chapter 5

Games for Teenagers (Ages 12-18)

Teenagers are notoriously difficult to reach. Their lives and minds are filled with distractions, identity crises, moral dilemmas, real-life safety concerns. They're often mopey or withdrawn. They tend to gravitate away from family activities as signifying a lifestyle they're trying to grow out of. And this is all perfectly natural and healthy.

If you've been playing this type of game with them since childhood, they may be a bit more open to it. It depends. So these games are designed to appeal to their advanced skill sets and lifestyle predispositions. Of course, you can't second-guess everybody, certainly not all at once.

Retention:

This is a great exercise for teenagers, as it is designed for their level of mental development. It works well for one person or more. If you have more than one, have them work as a team.

Find a suitable short story. No longer than one thousand words (about two pages or a bit more). There are stories for just this kind of thing online. Read it first yourself and prepare a list of questions (with the answers) about the details in the story. They can be multiple-choice, or they can be open-ended; that's up to you.

At gametime, have the team (or the solo participant) read the story once. Have them turn the paper over when they're done reading it the first time. Let them take as much time as is reasonable.

Then ask the team the questions. Give them time to search their memories. If it's a team, take note that each may often remember the same details differently, different colors or objects or quantities or other things. Keep note of the details they're listing and who is listing them.

After the exercise, read the questions and then the actual answers according to your key. Note the differences in patterns. Who was most often right, if anyone? Who was most often wrong? This will reflect strongly on their active listening skills (which entails retention, as we recall from our game of *Telephone*).

It also engages the kids in a shared goal, each one stimulating the others' memory. This is a competition the younger kids might just win, or at least they should make a good showing. After the answer part of the exercise, discuss:

Did they work together, or did they quarrel? Did they stick to their guns no matter how wrong they were? (That's known as the Dunning Kreuger effect.) Did they get frustrated by being contradicted? Those are narcissistic traits, things to watch out for in case they develop from tendencies to behaviors and finally to disorders.

If you have kids, what emotions did they feel working together? How did they feel when their memory wasn't accurate? Was it discouraging, frustrating? Well, they can rest assured that if they listen more actively, they will retain more. That's a lesson, like so many of these, which will last a lifetime and benefit them every day of that lifetime.

What emotions did you feel watching them work together?

Introduce Yourself (Roast-Style):

Here's a spin on the supportive introductory speech we tried with younger kids. This time, we'll add a double twist. First, we'll make it a roast. Instead of being strictly supportive, the introduction will include jibes meant with love. It may come across as a litany of insults and dirty jokes (you won't be doing either), but it is really just an affectionate lampoon. It's a Hollywood tradition, folks.

The problem is that this can easily hurt somebody's feelings, and that's not what we're trying to do here. In fact, you'll notice that these games are designed to avoid such unnecessary conflicts. They're all about building and strengthening bonds, not weakening or disintegrating them.

So instead of roasting one another, this game entails the speaker to roast themselves! They should be kind but fair, not afraid to laugh at themselves (which is a big part of this invaluable exercise and hilarious game). It requires self-awareness, a huge part of emotional intelligence. It also requires a certain tolerance to teasing, which is also a big part of EI. If you can't laugh at yourself, you shouldn't laugh at anybody else.

Everybody should know their own weaknesses. This is how we set about to proactively change our behavior and improve ourselves, another big part of EI. This exercise is practically emotional intelligence personified.

Here's a trick: Don't refer to yourself in the first person (I, me, mine) and use the third person, as if you were introducing somebody else (and that person is you). Make sure to do it with humor and self-sympathy, mentioning the speaker's own good points as well as weaknesses. Always remain in your own corner. Here's a little example for you, the game leader, to start things off:

"Thank you, folks. You all know your next guest needs no introduction ... but they're paying me anyway, so what the heck? Our next guest is truly outstanding in their field, and maybe she should have stayed out there! She's a loving mother, but sometimes she gets a little tense. Somebody told her once that she was too tense; she answered, 'No, but I do have reservations.' She drives her kids to school ... then at home, she drives them crazy! She's so proud of her kids. Her kids claim to love her cooking, but they seem to love feeding the dog even more! Seriously, folks. She was nominated to be Mother of the Year ... that was in another lifetime, but still ... sometimes it's hard to tell! She's a great provider in her own right though ... she gives her husband headaches almost every night!"

And so on. Have fun with it. End with some backpedaling compliments to keep things light:

"Seriously though, here's a person I've known my whole life, and I'm confident that nothing is going to come between us. She's known by a lot of names, Mom, Honey, Hey You, Watch Where You're Driving ... But I feel privileged to be the only one who can call her ... me."

Introduce yourself, lap up the applause, take your bow, and sit down. If you've done well, you've set a great example that any kid can follow. They list their interests, claim to be bad at them, then say a few nice things and boom, they're done. It's great for self-esteem because to laugh at yourself brings tremendous personal security. It's something narcissists can't do well, so it's an important skill to master young.

This skill will help your children avoid teasing of any sort, or bullying. Those things are confounded by unexpected reactions. The teasing person expects upset; the bully expects fear. Join the bully in making fun of yourself, then you have defeated them. Show no fear of the bully, and you have done the same thing. The bully challenges you to a fight; answer with a few self-deprecating remarks, and you'll leave them stunned and stunted, and will walk away the stronger, better person.

Enjoy the other presentations. Laugh enthusiastically, applaud and cheer, and share this little bit of humble pie. It's a bittersweet confection, but it really goes down smooth.

Continue The Story:

This one's great for kids of all ages, but older kids will have a better grip on it, as this takes a sharp wit and keen, developed mind. It's pretty self-explanatory, and can be done with a group of two or more. Set a rotation, and start it with something like:

"Peter went to the store to buy some ice cream. On the way there, he met ..." Now point to the next participant and let them take up the narrative:

"His friend Tim, who was going to the bowling alley next to the ice cream shop."

Let the story develop naturally from there. It's a great exercise for the imagination, active listening, understanding of character and circumstance. Try to squeeze as much emotion as you can into your part of the narrative and see how it plays out. Do the others abandon the emotion in favor of a reasoned but dispassionate story? Do they introduce emotions of their own?

And even EI tells us that there's more to life than emotion. What choices are they making for their characters, their lives, their fates? Do they go to dark places with their story of the ice cream and bowling expedition, or are they comical? Perhaps they tell a story of peaceful resolution and minimal conflict. Remember that their contributions are very likely to have autobiographical aspects. That will tell you more about your teenager's perspective than any kind of direct conversation, that's for sure.

Emotional Taboo:

Here's one that may take a little preparation, but it's well worth it. All you need to play this is suitable cards, or lists of prohibited hints, and somebody to work the buzzer when one of those prohibited words (or a proper name or a rhyme) for the answer is used. So you need at least three people for this game. If you have five or more (in odd numbers), you can have competing teams.

Your emotion card will list the emotion in question, and (in this case) four clues the person cannot give. For example:

(answer): Anger

(prohibited clues): Mad, Fists, Fury, Hate

You also could not use *(blank) Management*, as this is the proper name of a TV show and movie. You can't use *hanger* either, as it's a rhyme. Usable clues might include: *Not frustration, but ..., When I was at that party and drank too much ...* You can use tone of voice as well.

It'll take a little time and creativity to come up with these cards (you may want to use cardstock, so buy some of that along with a good pair of scissors). In addition to emotions, you can include traits (frugal, talkative). That will provide you with as many answers as you could possibly need. If you need more, simply expand the categories to your taste. Keep them in the behavioral cycle (emotion, thought, action).

Emotional Password:

The old gameshow Password seems to be getting new life on The Tonight Show Starring Jimmy Fallon, so it's one teenagers may know. It can work for only two people or more. If you have four or any higher even number, break them up into competing teams of two. In each team, one person knows the password and tries to get the other to guess it using only one other word as a clue. The person has a limited time to guess before it goes to the next team. Proper names are allowed (unlike *Emotional Taboo*) but miming is not. To keep this version challenging, synonyms are not allowed. All teams are given the same password.

A big part of the game is to pay attention to the previous, failed word clues, combining them to find the answer. Here's a quick example:

(The password is *space*)

Team 1

Clue: Empty ...

Guess: Cupboards.

Team 2

Clue: Outer ...

Guess: Space.

It's a fun game which requires active listening, reason over emotion, and other things we're developing here. The key is to put the word in some kind of context. Our version, of course, will have emotions or related traits as the passwords. Such as:

(The password is *happy)*

Team 1

Clue: ... Days.

Guess: Happy.

It's really more challenging than you think, so it needs a somewhat advanced intellect. And putting the emotions in context is great for emotional development. Here are a few more examples:

(The password is *frustrated)*

Clue: School

Clue: The office

Clue: Taxes

And so on. The more challenging the game is, the more effective and more rewarding as well.

Emotional Match Game:

This is another in a series of games inspired by classic game shows. This one made Richard Dawson (later of *Family Feud*) the star that he was. In this game, a classic joke is told minus one word out of the punchline. The contestant offers their choice, and six celebrities offer theirs. Each match is a one point out of six.

Here's an example:

> Joke: Audrey said, "I had no idea a costume party could be so dangerous. I went dressed as a potato, and somebody tried to _____ me." (Whoever reads the joke/question usually says *blank* during the blank.)
>
> Answers: peel, roast, slice'n'dice, bury, mash

Here's another:

> Joke: When Old Mrs. Periwinkle (funnier names work best) takes off her wig at night, she looks like _____."
>
> Answers: Patrick Stewart, Mr. Periwinkle, her own big toe, a mummy's grandmother, a bowling ball covered in turkey skin.

Remember that you're playing for a match though. It's not a funniest-punchline contest. Even the misses should get praise for creativity. In the first example, peel is the most obvious, but bury is the cleverer response.

There was also a round where a phrase was left blank, such as:

> Joke: _____ Sickness.
>
> Answers: Morning, sea, love, home, air

For our purposes, simply make emotions first and foremost in the setup, which itself a joke. Emotions are baked into comedy as it is, it's only a matter of bringing them out.

Joke: Mad Martin was so mad, he stormed out of the party without his ______.

Answers: Date, pants, dignity, friendships

Or:

Joke: Sally was so confused, she went to the Apple store for _______.

Answers: groceries, a Big Mac, an orange, good service, the bargain prices

It doesn't take much preparation. Spend a little time surfing the internet for jokes, find ones that include dumb (substitute *confused* for the sake of political correctness) or others you can twist around and use. Hey, jokes are a part of our shared oral tradition, and almost everybody likes a good joke, kids especially. You'll need paper and pens for every participant.

EMOTIONAL FAMILY FEUD:

Let's take this concept one step further, to one of the most beloved gameshows of all time. *Family Feud* took its name from the format of using teams of contestants and having those teams be real-life families.

But the crux of the game is about picking the most popular answer, much like *Match Game*. In the *Feud*, surveys ask a group of people to answer simple questions, and these are the standards by which the answers are ranked. For example:

> Question: *Things* you find in a bathroom
>
> Answers: Toothbrush, toilet, sink, shower, towels

Out of a hundred people, if 50 said toilet, that's the number-one answer and worth 50 points. Each member of the family or team plays against another member of the family or team. Three wrong guesses, or strikes, passes the round to the other team for a steal. There's also a lightning round with a slight variety on this motif.

The *Feud* (as it's called in Hollywood) is an ideal game for the workplace for a litany of reasons. But let's get back to the family.

For our purposes, you don't have to survey anyone. You're the survey. You pick the question and the five answers. You put together the questions, and of course you'll be sticking to emotions, traits, and related subjects. Here are a few examples:

> Question: *People* who make a person angry
>
> Answers: bosses, in-laws, politicians, bad neighbors, bad waiters

Or:

> Question: *Things* that make a person happy
>
> Answers: Puppies, big meals, toys, friends, jokes

Remember, you pick the answers, and they will provide the lessons you wish to teach. If you want to teach your kids that money will make them happy, let that be one of the answers you choose. If you want to teach them that friends are more important, pick that. They'll probably guess both things over the course of the round, but remember that a wrong guess is a strike.

And, unlike the famous '70s TV show, maybe not so much kissing the contestants.

Dub A Sitcom:

This is one for the quick-witted and witty. Sitcoms have several characteristics which make it perfect to turn the sound down and dub new dialogue from the couch. The storylines are often inconsequential, the emotions are broadly played, and they're mostly dialogue.

Prepare this the way you would an improv session. Pick a sitcom, and it doesn't have to be one everybody knows. That might help. But it can also have hysterical results if you don't. If you have six people, *Friends* might be a good choice. More than that? *The Office*. Fewer? Maybe *It's Always Sunny in Philadelphia*. Don't be afraid to cast men for women and women for men. The results can be naturally side-splitting. Avoid sitcoms with foul language, like *Veep* or *Trailer Park Boys*, and make one rule that no swearing is allowed by anyone (that means you too). As Groucho Marx said, "If you need to be dirty to be funny, then you're not funny." You'll have to explain to your kids who Groucho Marx was.

And it's always a great idea to keep the humor going in your household. It defuses tensions (which run high among teenagers) and encourages cooperation in the family (which runs low among teenagers).

After casting, pick a storyline. It's not supposed to be the storyline of the actual episode. Invent one, using this easy formula. (It works if you decide to write a sitcom too.)

A member of the cast is faced with a dilemma, and learns a lesson from others about how to solve it. Think about a few classic sitcom episodes:

- Hawkeye has to stay awake while stranded with a Korean family who don't speak English (*M*A*S*H*)

- Dennis sets about to write his memoirs, but the gang gets in the way (*It's Always Sunny ...*)
- Mary's professionalism is challenged by the death of a beloved children's entertainer (*The Mary Tyer Moore Show*)

It's not that tricky. Pick a character, a task, and let 'er rip. And since you're really not writing a sitcom episode (*on spec*, as they say in the biz), you don't have to worry about the narrative. It will be helpful, however, and rewarding.

Now play the episode and have fun. Don't be afraid to exaggerate the dialogue, especially the emotions. Play it to the hilt, ham it up (most TV actors do). Enjoy yourself.

This game has incredible benefits. It's extremely good for sharpening the sense of humor. It may bring out the hidden writer in your child (or in you). It requires an understanding of characters and circumstances and how they relate to emotions, and that's central to emotional intelligence, as you know.

During the commercial breaks, stop and chat about the story, the characters, and the jokes you or your family had come up with. Be generous with your praise, as this will only encourage more and better efforts. Do not denigrate anyone for anything. But you can sway them in one direction or the other.

This exercise can be especially revealing as to where your kids are in their development. Are they naturally funny? Do they have trouble thinking quickly? Do they find the challenge befuddling and frustrating, leading to outbursts? How did *you* do? Maybe you're not quite as clever or witty as you thought. Hey, who is?

Movie Night:

Granted, movies aren't technically games. But they are a great way to reach kids, teenagers included. And teenagers can be very hard to reach. The reason we're introducing movies at this stage, for teenagers (older teenagers too) is that these particular movies are hand-selected for the purpose of teaching emotional intelligence. And watching them and discussing them are fantastic family activities.

But these aren't Batman movies. These are intense dramas, recommended for mature viewers. These are gritty, realistic movies which confront the real-world dilemma of emotional intelligence. They're likely to bore some people. Others will be deeply engaged. They are very intense and may upset some viewers. Well, as provocative art, they're designed to do just that. But they're nothing a modern teenager can't digest, and there's no sexual content in any of them, so you don't have to worry about that. Who is or is not engaged, and how you and your family react to these particular films, will be quite telling of their worldviews and perspectives.

You might notice that the explanations are more involved than those of the previous exercises. This is intentional. Here, instead of a race game or a brief roleplay, you'll be spending a few hours at a time watching some very intense dramas. A detailed explanation will hopefully help to make the most of that time.

These are also movies which your older teenage children (maybe yourself too) have probably not seen, so this is a good opportunity to broaden your artistic horizons as you bond as a family. And if you're a fan of good movies, you'll thank me for the recommendations and share these movies with your friends too.

Watching the movies and discussing them go hand in hand. Don't do one without the other, for reasons you will come to understand. Anyway, it's in the discussing of the movies where you find the real revelations about yourself and your family, and where you'll create those strong bonds which will last long after the birds leave the nest.

These movies will become gradually more intense. We'll start off with the easy one.

BILLY BUDD (1962): This is an enduring film adaptation of Herman Melville's story of a virtuous young sailor's misadventure aboard a British warship around 1800. Despite being commonly interpreted as having homosexual themes, the story is a religious allegory, a retelling of the passion of the Christ. Billy Budd is the blameless Christ figure, the ship's Captain Veer stands in for Pontius Pilate, the wicked master-at-arms Claggart represents the Pharisees, and the crew stand in for the apostles.

What makes *Billy Budd* relevant to our purposes?

The movie is predicated on the concept of emotional intelligence. The wily Capt. Veer has a keen eye for what drives the men on his ship. Several references are made to this, and the character is often shot simply observing the other characters. The character visibly goes through the three steps of emotion, thought, then decision. You can see it in a scene when he scolds the men on deck, and in a private interview scene with Master-at-Arms Claggart regarding Billy Budd's supposed conspiracy to commit mutiny (spoiler alert).

The master-at-arms also has a keen sense of emotional intelligence, which he uses to manipulate Billy toward his doom.

Billy himself also exudes emotional intelligence, in a manner which parallels the master-at-arms, his adversary in the story. Billy is often seen refusing to be emotionally manipulated, responding instead with reason. Yet at times when emotion overwhelms him, he stutters terribly. This is when his emotional intelligence fails, and it is his great weakness.

So this is a movie about emotional intelligence; who uses it, how, why, and what price there is to pay for not having it.

After the film, which ends exquisitely, discuss it with your family. Could they have figured out a way to save Billy? What would they have done in Capt. Veer's shoes? Which characters among the crew did they find interesting and why? Do they see the allegorical parallel to the story of Jesus' trial and execution? What do they make of it?

'NIGHT, MOTHER (1986): Also an adaptation, of a Pulitzer Prize-winning play, this riveting film stars Sissy Spacek and Anne Bancroft in heartbreaking performances as a suicidal daughter and the mother who is desperate to save her. Like *Billy Budd, 'Night, Mother* is predicated on the principles of emotional intelligence. The daughter seems bereft of emotion, completely dead inside. This, actually, is the reason for her suicide. Cold reason tells her that life simply isn't worth living. Her mother, on the other hand, is seething with emotion: guilt, terror, desperation, confusion. Still, she tries to use reason to convince her daughter not to go through with her tragic intentions. The film is heart-wrenching.

And it's a valuable case in point in a lot of regards. Teen suicide is at an all-time high. Depression and substance abuse statistics are through the roof.

In 2018, suicide was the second-leading cause of death among 10- to 24-year-olds in the United States. Recent studies show that almost 20% of US high school students have seriously considered suicide. Almost nine percent have attempted suicide.

A lot of this stems from a lack of emotional intelligence. Despair is little more than unbridled emotion without the balance of reason. This is a film all parents should watch with their teenage children in this regard alone. And this is a film which must be discussed for that reason, to bring to the surface any burgeoning feelings of conflict which might manifest themselves horribly as time goes on.

It's also a fine lesson in how treacherous life can be, even a very simple life, when emotional intelligence is lacking. Emotion and reason must work together. One can hardly survive, much less thrive, without the other.

And, like *Billy Budd*, *'Night, Mother* poses the viewer a challenge, and something to discuss afterward. Was there anything anybody could have said or done to change Jessie's mind? What does it say about a person when, even though they are committed to reason over emotion, they still won't listen to reason? It happens more often than any of us would like to admit, and it's a big part of emotional intelligence.

A WOMAN UNDER THE INFLUENCE (1974): This gritty drama by writer/director John Cassavetes stars Peter Falk as a construction worker and Gena Rowlands as his eccentric wife and homemaker. Cassavetes is known for his brutally honest independent films of the '70s, and this film typifies that style. There are no comforting trappings of a Hollywood film. There's no score to speak of, no adorable romance. It can be a hard film to watch, but not because there's no score.

The film centers around the marital tensions between the characters played by husband Falk and wife Rowlands. He believes her eccentricities are leading her to a nervous breakdown. He tries to correct her behavior, but it only gets worse. Falk's character is so limited in his perspective, and his wife is so sympathetic in hers, that it makes the film a real challenge.

Clearly, it's the husband's behavior which is driving the wife to a breakdown. She's under the influence all right, of her husband.

Emotional intelligence is at the very heart of this film. Falk's character is lacking in emotional intelligence entirely. He is prone to fits of rage which he thinks are caused by his wife. But his anger is outsized for the circumstance. He has no control over himself, and he doesn't recognize that he has any problem at all (much less that he *is* the problem). He has a narcistic personality, likely disordered.

His wife, on the other hand, is extremely emotionally intelligent. Left to her own devices, she is well-adjusted, unconcerned about what others think of her. She is creative and lively and funny. She is fully functional and given to no abusive traits. She cannot quite express all this, so one could say her communications skills are lacking. Her husband's are as well. But if he had any emotional intelligence at all, he'd see that. The film is a harrowing look at what happens when emotional intelligence is lacking in a marital relationship, and it's a great cautionary tale.

And, like the others, this is a film which must be discussed in order to have practiced this exercise responsibly. What do your teenagers make of the husband, the wife? Note what your daughter makes of the husband, what your son makes of the wife, not just how they interpret the characters of their own gender. It says a lot about how much they're programmed to expect or accept in a marriage. This is a good opportunity to refresh your children about boundaries, abusive relationships, narcissism, and, of course, emotional intelligence.

In addition, writer Paul Schrader gives us two films steeped in emotional intelligence, *TAXI DRIVER* (1976) and *AFFLICTION* (1997). Both are stories of men who lack emotional intelligence entirely. They fail to get along in society, to maintain intimate relationships, to control their own violent tempers.

Movies are a great way to bring the family together for an intensive look at emotional intelligence. Be on the lookout for other stories of this sort, to keep EI movie night going strong!

And that brings us to the end of this chapter, and to the bulk of the book. Or does it? We have one more chapter for you, to make sure the emotional intelligence of your whole family remains strong, in this generation and for generations to come.

PART THREE

PLUS . . .

Chapter 6

Other Options

Hopefully, you've enjoyed the games you've played with your family. You've probably noticed a lot of concrete progress in your family unity, as well as your mutual and individual emotional intelligence. That will serve you all well in every facet of your life, especially interacting with one another.

But there are lots of ways you can have fun with your family and still instill these vital lessons. They're not limited to emotional intelligence either. There are games which will teach you and your family leadership skills, people-reading, communications skills, and more.

And all of these things can be developed in a variety of ways. Once you're ready to take it past the living room or the backyard, there are lots of fun things outside the home to take your family's development even further.

For kids, organized team sports are a tremendous way to master emotional intelligence, communications skills, socials skill, leadership skills, and much more. Every study points to greater success for kids who participate in group sports. It naturally instills in them the necessity of thought disciplining emotion, understanding others, active listening, empathy, integrity, and everything that makes a reliable, admirable, and well-adjusted adult.

Take your family to a park and organize a game of your own. Capture the Flag is a good organized activity for a family, and these types of competitive events have natural benefits for developing emotional intelligence, as we've seen. Losing can be a learning opportunity which a whole generation seems to have missed out on; perhaps that was our generation. And losing to your kids is a great way to develop your own emotional intelligence, not to mention humility.

Take your family to museums and zoos, whatever your ideological stance on the latter. Art is designed to appeal to emotion, in ways the intellect doesn't often understand. You've touched on this in the games you played at home, but this takes the principle to the next level. A zoo is an experience you cannot duplicate at home, despite being able to use pictures of animals, as you already have done. How does seeing the animals affect your kids? How does it affect you? It's different seeing them move and react to their surroundings. You can watch footage on the internet, but this is also a great, old-fashioned activity, especially for young kids. You may want to leave the teenagers at home for that one.

Take your kids to a big musical presentation of some kind. It may be a rock concert, if you both can find something the other can stand. It may be a musical production that's in town, even a small theater production (as long as it has music). A symphony will work too. The main thing is to sit them down in front of a controlled piece of music which is intended to generate emotion. And even for the most jaded teenager, a show like *The Lion King* or *The Producers* can be quite entertaining. Afterward, you'll want to discuss the event, especially as it regards their emotional reactions to key points. Where the music was at its most dramatic will be where the emotion was at its highest pitch, as you can easily imagine. Were they affected? Were they left nonplussed? At the very least, it's an opportunity to take your family out for a night at the theater, and how often do any of us do that these days? We're more apt to leave the kids with a sitter if we can score tickets to something like *Hamilton* in the first place.

Taking your kids to a sporting event can have the same benefit. This is a family activity which hardly needs our endorsement. The sports families out there are already benefiting from the emotional intelligence and family bonding which sharing a favorite team or sport can provide.

And make sure to discuss it afterward, as others might talk about a movie or concert. How about that play? What about that strategy? How about those cheerleaders?

Consider an escape room for a fun activity with your family (especially effective for your work team if you're crossing these activities over to that realm). They have simple versions for children and families, and it's a great way to challenge yourselves. Fear and wonder and other emotions will certainly arise (that's how these things are designed), so it's a great way to challenge ourselves and each other emotionally, discovering how we will really react to unusual circumstances, learning to process feelings into thoughts and then into actions, allowing reason to trump emotion, and other vital skills we've learned here.

And you probably won't be surprised that, when it comes to emotional intelligence, they've got an app for that. In fact, they've got several, and each specializes in a slightly different offering:

Smiling Mind is a meditation-based app which offers:

- Guided meditations which get increasingly longer
- Emotion tracking before and after sessions
- Offline activities which can be used in or out of the classroom

Mood Meter helps users recognize their own emotions and offers:

- Cause tracing
- Mood control
- Positivity training

Mitra also helps users track emotions and their values as well. It offers:

- Emotion and values rating
- Priority tracking and measuring
- Change tracking

Stop, Breathe & Think is another meditations-based app which offers:

- Meditations based on how the user is feeling
- Progress tracking
- Graphs to illustrate emotional trends

Discovering Emotions with Zeely is for younger users or students who are on the autism spectrum. This makes deciphering and managing emotions extremely difficult. This app offers:

- Help learning to read facial expressions
- Help learning to recognize feelings
- Cute cartoon characters

Social Adventures is also great for young kids, especially those with social skills challenges. Social skills and emotional intelligence are very closely related, and a discrepancy in one indicates discrepancy in another. This app offers a wide variety of activities and games.

Character Playbook is designed for middle school-aged and high school-aged students. It focuses on social relationships and offers:

- Comic book-esque stories to guide students through everyday situations
- Modules with quizzes
- Progress assessment
- *Calm* is great for users of all ages. It offers:
- Meditations
- Breathing exercises
- Help falling asleep

Apps lead us to a brief discussion of video games. For all the talk of how dangerous video games may or may not be, a new study shows that they can actually be beneficial in the quest for greater emotional intelligence, particularly among teens.

Results clearly showed an improvement in emotional expression and evaluation as regards their own feelings. It didn't seem to last over several months, but since kids who play video games rarely let up, that should lead to consistently higher levels. The study also found that cognitive revaluation (part of active listening) was more often used as a strategy of emotional regulation, and that result increased over time.

There are also lots of games you can buy for kids to play with one another, if you still want to go that route. We don't claim to be the only source of games about emotional intelligence, of course. But we do strive to be the best. We encourage you to try a few others though, and let us know what kind of success you have.

CONCLUSION

Has the end come already? Well, time flies (and so do pages) when you're having fun. You and your family have certainly learned a lot on this little journey. Let's take a moment to reflect on that.

We've covered a whole semester of a psyche's worth of emotional intelligence information. You've been reminded of games you haven't played in years and learned a bunch of new ones. You've picked up ideas for the home, the workplace, and hopefully have become inspired to look for new opportunities to become more aware of yourself and your surroundings and to help others do the same.

Hopefully, you've discovered a way to communicate with your kids, a new way of seeing them and perhaps of seeing yourself. You're also now up-to-date on the latest apps and EI technology, as far as it goes.

Did you recognize a lot of these games? You've seen several on TV, and others may be familiar from schoolrooms and living rooms across the country and all over the planet. Did you ever imagine *The Hokey Pokey* could ever be so psychologically potent?

Did you learn anything about yourself, about your triggers and how to deal with them? What did your kids learn most notably? What lessons got by them? What's the plan to try again so those lessons sink in? Remember, it's not enough just to note a problem, certainly not to excuse it. It must be corrected for a socially grounded individual to have a well-adjusted psyche.

What did you find most surprising? Had you ever seen a Cassavetes film, or even heard of *Billy Budd* (outside that one episode of *The Sopranos*)? Have you ever tried dubbing a sitcom before? That's something you're just not allowed to do (talking during a show is very rude) and it's nice to have license to misbehave every now and then. If you understand that, then your sense of emotional intelligence is indeed elevated. We'd like to take a little credit for that, but you deserve most of it. You saw a problem, you identified it, and you took steps to correct it. And you did it in a creative way, not afraid of old-fashioned approaches. These are age-old problems, after all. Family movie might (or family game night for that matter) may seem like old-fashioned ideas (because they are). How did they go over in your household? Did your older kids balk? Did the younger kids shine? Maybe it was the other way around. You really can't know what's going to happen with these things until you do them.

And you can do them more than once. Most of these games can be played several times. You may want to return to one or more of them in times of emotional crisis. You may want to have an emotional check-in with your kids from time to time, even if there is no emotional crisis at all. You may want to do the same with your spouse or even yourself. As we said early on, it's important to be mindful of these things throughout our lives. It's all too easy to become sloppy with our own emotions and inattentive to the emotions of others. Preventing that is what emotional intelligence is all about.

You can also use these games to inspire you to think of your own games. Feel free to tweak these as you deem necessary and fitting. No two people are the same, no two families are the same, and no two circumstances are the same.

We hope you found the instructions easy to follow and the games fun to play. We hope you appreciated the dribs and drabs of comedy sprinkled throughout. In a book about fun, we hope we made the reading fun too.

You may also find that the approach works so well, you'd like to take it to the next step. As we've discussed, EI is one set of skills among many, and they all work in tandem. Leadership skills, communications skills, social skills, reading people, and other skill sets can all be learned and developed in the same way EI can be, and using similar techniques. We'll be publishing (or may already have, depending on when you're reading this) a whole series of books along these lines. They have the same all-killer-no-filler technical information, as well as fun and inventive approaches to personal development and family bonding, good for the Whole Family.

And by *whole family*, of course, we mean more than a reference to our series' brand. Whole family, as we've learned, is one of the few modern true-to-form paradoxes in the English language. There are many fractured families these days, and that trend is only getting worse. Fractured families beget fractured families, a generational inheritance which is a true threat to the American social landscape. But, with mastery of EI and other skill sets, you can have a whole family. The top-quality line of *Your Whole Family* books and games is committed to this idea, and we will always be here to make you, and your family, more whole, to help you bring mind, body, and soul together in complete wholeness and total wellness.

Good luck and have fun!

Thank you for reading.

If you enjoyed this book, please take a few moments to write a review on your favorite store.

RESOURCES

STATISTICS:

Marriage And Family Therapist Statistics and Facts In The US. (n.d.) Retrieved from *https://www.zippia.com/marriage-and-family-therapist-jobs/demographics/*

Marriage and Family Therapy: Statistics and Data. (n.d.). Retrieved from https://libguides.usc.edu/c.php?g=316355&p=2113360

Marriage and Family Therapists. (n.d.). Retrieved from https://datausa.io/profile/soc/marriage-and-family-therapists

GENERAL:

Daniel Goleman. (1998). *Working with Emotional Intelligence.*

Lauren Landry. (2019, April 03). *Why Emotional Intelligence Is Important In Leadership.* Retrieved from https://online.hbs.edu/blog/post/emotional-intelligence-in-leadership

Emotional Intelligence in Leadership. (n.d.). Retrieved from https://www.mindtools.com/pages/article/newLDR_45.htm

Dori Meinert. (2018, February 23). *Emotional Intelligence Is Key to Outstanding Leadership*. Retrieved from https://www.shrm.org/hr-today/news/hr-magazine/0318/pages/emotional-intelligence-is-key-to-outstanding-leadership.aspx

Gerald Ainomugisha. (n.d.). *The Importance of Emotional Intelligence in Leadership*. Retrieved from https://inside.6q.io/emotional-intelligence-in-leadership/

Dave Clark. (2018, April 24). *Important Distinctions Between EQ and IQ*. Retrieved from https://blog.ttisi.com/important-distinctions-between-eq-and-iq

Kendra Cherry. (2020, November 19). *Is IQ or EQ More Important?* Retrieved from https://www.verywellmind.com/iq-or-eq-which-one-is-more-important-2795287

Justin Bariso. (n.d.). *Why EQ Matters More Than IQ Because no man (or woman) is an island*. Retrieved from https://www.inc.com/justin-bariso/why-eq-matters-more-than-iq.html

Examples of Emotional Intelligence. (2020, May 14). Retrieved from https://harappa.education/harappa-diaries/examples-of-emotional-intelligence-in-the-workplace

Linda Lantieri. (2001, February 22). *A View on Emotional Intelligence in Everyday Life*. Retrieved from https://www.edutopia.org/linda-lantieri-emotional-intelligence-everyday-life

Berrett-Koehler. (2018, September 11). *The Importance of Emotional Intelligence in a Leader*. Retrieved from https://medium.com/@BKpub/the-importance-of-emotional-intelligence-in-a-leader-d1ffc7fd753c

Christopher Dollard. (n.d.). *The Emotional Intelligence Is Key to Successful Leadership*. Retrieved from https://www.gottman.com/blog/emotional-intelligence-key-successful-leadership/

Emotional Intelligence in Leadership. (n.d.). Retrieved from https://www.managementcentre.co.uk/learning-development/emotional-intelligence-leadership/

Erickson Coaching International. (2016, August 08) *The Five Pillars of Emotional Intelligence*. Retrieved from https://erickson.edu/blog/five-pillars-of-emotional-intelligence

Kobi Simmat. (2019, October 3). *The Five Pillars of Emotional Intelligence. Retrieved from* https://www.linkedin.com/pulse/five-pillars-emotional-intelligence-kobi-simmat/

Gini Beqiri. (2018, September 9). *The 5 Features of Emotional Intelligence*. Retrieved from https://virtualspeech.com/blog/5-features-emotional-intelligence

Christopher D. Connors. (2018, June 1). *The 10 Qualities of an Emotionally Intelligent Person*. Retrieved from https://medium.com/personal-growth/the-10-qualities-of-an-emotionally-intelligent-person-f595440af4fb

Power of Positivity. (2021, April 12). *13 Qualities of People with High Emotional Intelligence*. Retrieved from https://www.powerofpositivity.com/qualities-people-high-emotional-intelligence/

John Rampton. (n.d.). *10 Qualities of People With High Emotional Intelligence. If you want to know if you have high emotional intelligence, here are a few tips to guide you along the way.* Retrieved from https://www.inc.com/john-rampton/10-qualities-of-people-with-high-emotional-intelligence.html

Justin Bariso. (n.d.). *13 Signs of High Emotional Intelligence. Wonder what emotional intelligence looks like in everyday life? Here are 13 examples*. Retrieved from https://www.inc.com/justin-bariso/13-things-emotionally-intelligent-people-do.html

Heather Craig. (2022, February 4). *17 Emotional Intelligence Tests and Assessments*. Retrieved from https://positivepsychology.com/emotional-intelligence-tests/

Emotional intelligence - Can You Measure It? (2002, July 1). Retrieved from https://www.hrmagazine.co.uk/article-details/emotional-intelligence-can-you-measure-it

Emotional Intelligence Measures. (n.d.). Retrieved from http://www.eiconsortium.org/measures/measures.html

Peter J. O'Connor, Andrew Hill, Maria Kaya, and Brett Martin. (2019, May 28). *The Measurement of Emotional Intelligence: A Critical Review of the Literature and Recommendations for Researchers and Practitioners*. Retrieved from https://www.ncbi.nlm.nih.gov/pmc/articles/PMC6546921/

Testing Emotional Intelligence. (n.d.). Retrieved from http://www2.psych.utoronto.ca/users/reingold/courses/intelligence/cache/testing_ei.htm